VERWOC

VILLAGE TO TOWN

WRITTEN AND COMPILED BY JILL COULTHARD
WITH THE INVALUABLE HELP OF PAM REEKS
AND MEMBERS OF THE COMMUNITY
LINE DRAWINGS BY CLIVE DANIELS

DEDICATED TO

THE PEOPLE OF VERWOOD – PAST, PRESENT AND FUTURE

It is hoped that the stories and photographs contained in these pages will not only bring back memories to older residents but provide a source of interest to comparative newcomers to Verwood and those whose families lived here in past days.

We owe tremendous thanks to those residents, past and present, who have shared their memories and photographs to record the history of our ever-growing town. These have contributed greatly to the extensive archive collection of Verwood Historical Society.

Front Cover:	**Verwood Crossroads looking west in 2002** **Inset – A similar view in the early 20th century**
Back Cover:	**Verwood Church of England School**

J&JC PUBLICATIONS

First Published in 2007 by J&JC Publications

Millbrook, Station Road, Verwood, Dorset. BH31 7PU

ISBN 978-0-9556614-0-2

Graphic Design and Layout by John and Jill Coulthard

Printed by
Reprint, Alderholt, Dorset. SP6 3AA

Profits from the sale of this book will be distributed between
Verwood Historical Society and Verwood Heathland Heritage Centre

CONTENTS

VILLAGE TO TOWN

AN OVERVIEW

The fortunes of Verwood have ever been dependent on its underlying geology, the main characteristic of which is the acidic nature of its heathlands with resultant poor agricultural soil away from the more fertile alluvial valley of the River Crane.   Lying on the fringes of neighbouring great estates, it was of little importance to the major landowners and so gave rise to random immigration and settlement which would not have been tolerated in more traditionally structured villages.   It is this factor also which led to it being designated as suitable for the mass development and housing we see today.

The very nature of being isolated from day to day contact with a formal estate society produced a self-reliant breed of independent cottagers many of whom utilised the products of the heathland to make a basic living in such unpromising terrain.

Verwood is situated in the Hampshire Basin and on the south-western fringe of the New Forest.   Romford, on the western edge, is within the London Clay belt.   This area was mostly given up to woodland, pasture and arable farming where wheat, barley and oats were grown and later two brickyards were established.   The River Crane, here equidistant from the formerly important market towns of Cranborne and Ringwood, also provided a convenient watering place for horses and stock.

Much of Verwood has a sandy soil, being part of the Bagshot Beds.   It is a light, buff colour quartz-sand giving a wild, heathy landscape.   A vein of strong clay attracted many potters from the very earliest days as well as providing a ready made source of building material.   A narrow outcrop of Bracklesham Beds occurs at Ebblake on the Hampshire-Dorset border, where the soil is alternating clay and sand.   This clay produced distinctive white bricks used as decorative features on many local buildings.   Another brickyard was situated halfway between Ebblake and the centre of Verwood on a clay seam at Black Hill.

Plateau gravels are found at Redman's Hill, Pistle Down and Wedge Hill.   Valley gravel occurs in the Lower Common area at Potterne and Three Legged Cross, a few feet above the river alluvium.

Living in busy, bustling, ever-growing Verwood, it is perhaps hard to reconcile it with Cranborne doctor and historian Wake Smart's description of the area as

"an extensive tract of heathy land, of a wild and desolate aspect"

only the commons within the village giving a hint to its underlying nature but this observation was undoubtedly true, even into the early twentieth century.

Heathland is not a natural but a man-made environment resulting from the felling of native woodland.   In olden times it was managed by the grazing of animals and removal of its products for everyday use.   It is a vanishing feature of the Dorset landscape and Verwood is fortunate to have some fine examples within its boundaries.   Its products are no longer used in the pottery, brick making, broom making and farming industries but its habitat provides a home for Smooth Snakes, Sand Lizards and Dartford Warblers and it remains a peaceful place for country walks away from the now busy centre.

Thomas Hardy's most evocative descriptions of the bleak but beautiful Dorset heathlands are found in his novel "Return of the Native" and though set further west may give us a vivid impression of the way our countryside appeared in those less crowded times when it was possible to walk from Poole to Christchurch with scarcely a dwelling in sight.

This book seeks to recount how Verwood grew from a series of scattered hamlets through village status to the present town and to provide an insight into the many and varied aspects of its people and their lives.

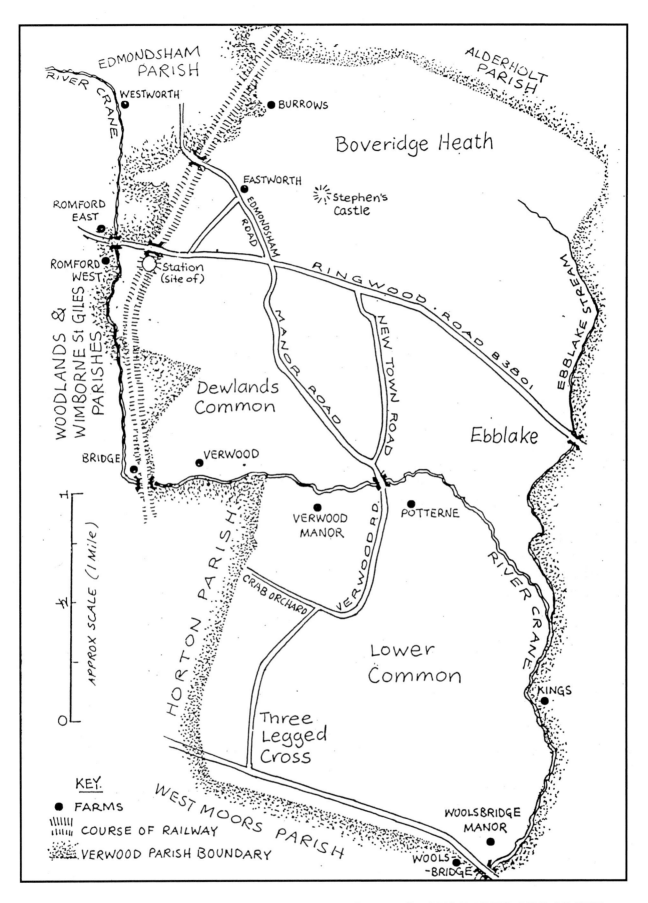

VERWOOD PARISH BOUNDARIES WITH CONTIGUOUS PARTS OF DORSET

TO THE EAST IS ALSO THE COUNTY BOUNDARY WITH HAMPSHIRE

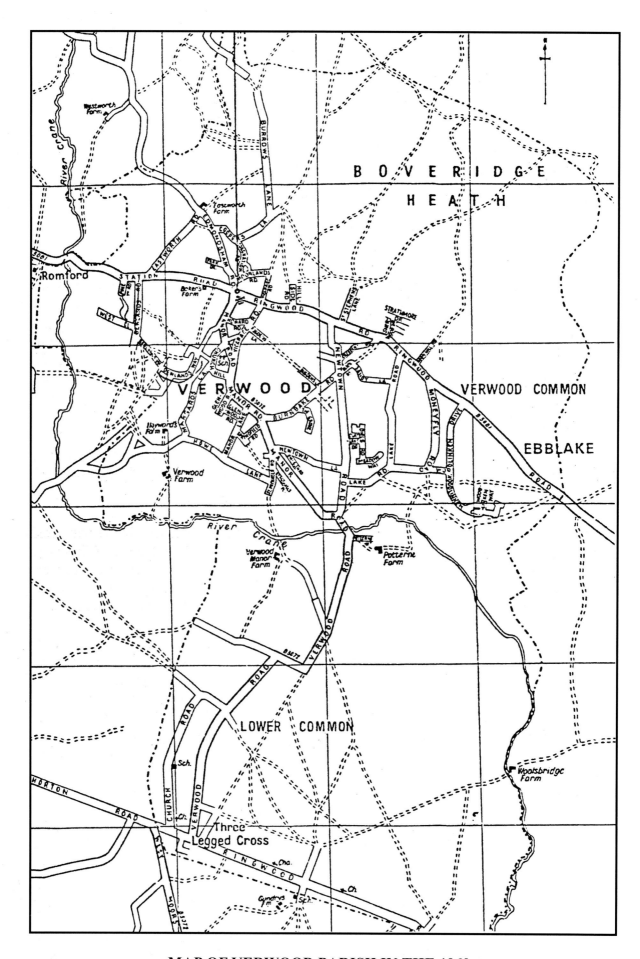

MAP OF VERWOOD PARISH IN THE 1960s

THE EARLY YEARS

The Road to Eastworth from Verwood, early twentieth century

Verwood was never a typical village grouped around a long established church with fields spreading beyond, but in the early days, just an outlying, unimportant hamlet of Cranborne with Romford, Three Legged Cross and Eastworth as separate tiny communities. Eastworth and Westworth were originally known as manors under one title of Horsych, later becoming Worth and are documented from the 13th century as is Romford whose name derives from a ford marked with a pole.

Although there have been settlements here since prehistoric times, the earliest actual remains of occupation are fragments of Tudor construction in some of the farmhouses. However, evidence of much older occupation is derived from the numerous barrows or burial mounds all over the surrounding area. Those in Verwood, mostly to the north east, are now obscured by Forestry land but in 1828 a barrow opened on Stephen's Castle, the high ground surmounting the sandpits to the north of Ringwood Road, contained an inverted unfired burial urn with fragments of burned bones and in the same year on Pistle Down, four beautifully chipped arrow heads were found.

In 1940 at the highest point of Boveridge Heath, men of the Royal Observer Corps constructing a "dug out" from where to observe enemy action, found a one and a half gallon earthenware urn containing human bones and close beside this a brick on which a crucifix was indented. A year earlier, workmen digging footings for a house in Edmondsham Road had found a late Bronze Age Socketal axe. These finds were taken to the County Museum in Dorchester.

The Forestry Commission who planted this area of former heathland in the 1920s ploughed out the barrows but although comparisons of soil have been sent for analysis and no deviations found, it is a mysterious fact that nothing will grow on the sites of these burial mounds. Some of these tumuli were known as Robin Hood's Butts because of their use as targets when archery was universally practised.

THE EARLY YEARS

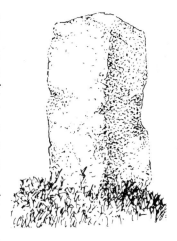

A landmark of ancient days was a Boundary marker of Cranborne Chase. Called the Wur or Hoare Stone" (hoare meaning boundary) it stood somewhere between Ebblake and Ringwood but its exact location is no longer known. Wake Smart tells us that many years ago the local inhabitants regarded the stone with a sort of superstitious reverence and told long tales about the impossibility of removing it. He may have been confusing this with "Stephen's Stone", a huge block of sandstone some 20 feet long, 10 feet wide and 9 feet high much further east on Boveridge Heath. This was meant to have had a golden casket buried underneath, as attributed to many similar stones, but despite attempts to raise it the casket, if it ever existed, has never been found. After lying buried for many years, in 1994 as part of the parish centenary celebrations and in partnership with the Parish Council and Verwood Historical Society it was partly excavated by Forest Enterprise as a feature and a pathway created.

The name "Stephen" associated with this part of Verwood may possibly be a folk memory of some ancient Chieftain who held sway in these parts. Stephen's Lane has now been given a prefix in deference to the Saint but this was not originally the case

Other quaintly named areas of Boveridge Heath are Mount Ararat and Wild Church Bottom. It has been suggested that the former name may have come from those times when non-conformist religion was particularly strong and now obscure biblical names were common. One compares the practice of naming Chapels Bethel, Zion, Bethesda and it is possible that, prior to any formal building, worshippers met together on the heath. Of Wild Church Bottom though Wake Smart said

"We cannot believe that a Christian Sanctuary ever reared its head on this lonely spot but if a worship of a people be traditionally recorded in the name, we would suppose that people to have been a colony of the original inhabitants of this country and this spot, the site of a Druidical temple or altar".

Although the great Ackling Dyke built by the Romans from Sorbiodunum (Old Sarum) to Vindocladia (Badbury Rings) runs some five miles to the west of Verwood, the only known evidence of Roman occupation in the parish yet discovered, is an oil lamp found in a garden at Three Legged Cross, though this of course was probably removed from its original site. However at nearby Horton a collection of pots and broken pottery dating from the first century B.C. was discovered together, with one hundred and thirty nine Roman coins and to the north west, Roman pottery and indications of a tesellated pavement were found in a meadow under Jordan's Hill off the Alderholt to Cranborne road.

The Saxons too, seem to have been slow to settle in the immediate area, put off from spreading west by the bleak heaths and repulsed as they approached from the north by the defences of Bokerley Ditch north of Cranborne. The Romano Britons who defied the Saxons, eventually fell back from Bokerley Ditch to Combs Ditch to the west, finally to be overrun by 650 A.D. It may be that anyone living in the Verwood area might have avoided the more unpleasant aspects of this conquest, managing to remain on the fringes. Some ancient British or 'Celtic' place names have survived in this area for example Pentridge but others such as Edmondsham, Gotham, Sutton, Horton and Mannington are apparently Saxon.

It seems likely too that the Parish boundaries, little changed since, were established certainly by the late Saxon period about 1000 years ago.

THE CONQUEST TO MONMOUTH

The Conquest saw William I appropriate the former Saxon stringent hunting rights of the area known as Cranborne Chase of which Verwood lay on the outer fringes. These rights were granted to and passed on by several noble families, at times reverting to the Crown and several monarchs hunted in the preserve. King John, likely the most frequent and enthusiastic royal visitor, did not own it as of right but through his first wife Isabella of Gloucester. How much these rights included and affected the people of Verwood is conjecture as will be later seen.

The Parish Church of St. Mary & St. Bartholomew, Cranborne, Dorset

From the first division of the country into parochial units, Verwood had been merely a scattered village in the vast parish of Cranborne with the smaller settlement of Three Legged Cross to the south being counted as part of its bounds. It remained such until it became an ecclesiastical parish in its own right in 1866 and part of the civil parish until 1894 so it is to Cranborne that we look for early documents.

The Domesday Book, commissioned in 1085, says "The King holds Creneburne". His own 'demesne' (land held for his own profit) included four mills worth 18s. It is possible that Holwell Mill, Romford Mill and one at Potterne were amongst these. The King also held 'Medesham' (Edmondsham) which a short time later appears to have consisted of four manors, the lord of one being called Beauboys or Bello Bosco.

THE CONQUEST TO MONMOUTH

In Old French or Latin this translates as beautiful or fair wood. In a charter dated December 8th 1377 William de Bello Bosco granted to Walter, Vicar of Cranborne amongst others

"all the lands, tenements, meadows, woodland, heath, marsh, pasture, rents and services which he then had in Lesteford, Fairwoode and Boverige".

Rev. John Hutchins, the great Dorset historian, suggests that the family derived its name from their place of residence and if he is correct in this it means that Fairwood, from the Old English "Faeger Wudu", was already the common name even before the Conquest. He quotes a case of a Norman family taking the surname Edmondsham, and it seems probable that Fairwood was similarly adopted but gave a more literal translation.

The charter was sealed at Fairwood which infers that members of the family may have resided here as well as holding lands, but even if so, we shall doubtless never know just where was the Bello Bosco's own House; one just has to imagine the feastings and jollifications, the training of the local peasantry in arms, the servants and farm workers. The arms of the Bello Bosco family, a chevron (inverted V) between three branches slipped, have been incorporated into the town's Coat of Arms.

The name "Beuboys" was recorded in 1288 and "Fairwod" in 1329 according to the Dictionary of English Place Names [A.D.Mills]. The name Fairwood persisted at least into the last century, side by side with other variations including Wirtwood, which was common in the 17th Century, and the one we recognise today – Verwood.

Fairwood was still retained at the railway station until its closure where although the "official" name Verwood was on the station signs, the more correct "Fairwood" was spelled out on the bank in flowers and pebbles. The variations and the final choice of Verwood are without due to the pronunciation of the old Dorset language. To be completely faithful to the Dorset tongue, we should pronounce the name of our village as "Ver'ood" or "Ver'ud". The present name is perhaps a good compromise between that and standard English!

As an aside at this point, many people have asked the origin of the name Three Legged Cross but to date it is not certain from when it was first so called. Explanations put forward include a tripod beacon which stood there to guide travellers across the heath, a gallows ("three legged mare") and a three sided stone marking the meeting of three great estates but a former County Archivist believed that the more prosaic reason is just the dog's leg arrangement of the junctions there.

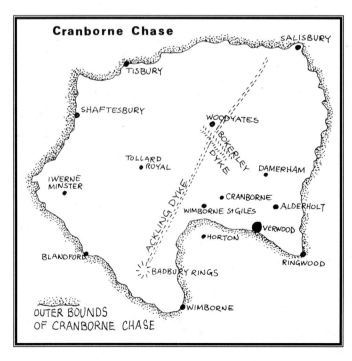

The outer bounds of Cranborne Chase covered a vast area, north-south from Wimborne to Salisbury and east-west from Shaftesbury to the edge of the New Forest along the banks of the River Avon. When King John established the actual boundaries of the Outer Chase, the line ran from Wimborne up the Allen valley to Stanbridge. The bracketed names are those given by Hutchins as his version of the original - *"to Longham Hayam (the long hedge or inclosure) which leads to Muledich...to King's ... by the way which leads to Esteford, through the middle of Estewode (Eastworth)...by the water of Cranborne to La Horewyeth (the hoar withy) to Albeslake (Ebblake)...to le Horeston (the hoar stone) ... to the great bridge by the way to Ringeswode (Ringwood)..."*

THE CONQUEST TO MONMOUTH

As can be seen, the precise line of the bounds as it runs through Verwood is now obscure as some of the place names have died out. The location of the ford at Esteford which appears elsewhere as Lesteford is particularly puzzling. In documents, it is said to be "Juxta (adjoining) Verwood" and is obviously somewhere on the River Crane, but precisely where would give a better indication of how much of the area actually fell within the Chase bounds. However there are several clues which lead us to place it at or near the present Bridge Farm on Horton Way.

In 1618 a number of maps were prepared as evidence over disputed bounds. Hardinge,'s map used by Wake Smart and subsequently Hutchins shows the line as sweeping north through Eastworth, cutting across the Crane not following it as the written perambulation states. Aldwell's map prepared for Lord Salisbury, though, is much more in agreement. It shows the bounds leaving the Allen at Stanbridge, continuing slightly northwards and turning east towards Woodlands (the lane into Woodlands from this road is called Kings Lane today), skirting Woodlands Park to the north through Kinges (King's Wood now to the north was probably more extensive in those days) and Estwood (an East Wood, now disappeared), reaching the Crane in the area of Bridge Farm, following the water round to the confluence of the Crane and Ebblake Stream where there is a withy bed at the point where the river joins the old parish and county boundary (hoar withy) and thence north to Ebblake.

Further evidence could be that Esteford was at different times held by the owners of Woodlands Park and Manor Farm. Bridge Farm lies between them. The Crane crossing near Bridge Farm was also known in earlier years as Verwood Ford, Verwood in those days lying more to the south of what we consider the centre today and, marked on maps as such, it must have been an important crossing place. If this surmise is correct, all the northern half of the present parish would have been within the outer bounds.

Another royal visit came about when the young King Edward VI in the last summer of his life in 1552 sat beneath an oak tree at Remedy Gates, Sutton to "touch for the King's Evil" which was believed to cure scrofula, a tubercular complaint. On 21st August he arrived at Woodlands for a three day stay in passage from Christchurch to Salisbury. The court procession must have been a magnificent sight and one wonders through which part of Verwood or Three Legged Cross it approached and how many villagers witnessed its progress. However the visit was not able to be universally enjoyed as plague was prevalent in the neighbourhood at the time and

"the country people were effectually restricted from anything like the loyal demonstrations of happier times" "by a proclamation to avoyde all manner of persons infected with pestilence or other contagious diseases.....to resorte to the courte at Woodlands during his Majesty's abode theare"

At the beginning of the 17th Century James I granted the Chase to Robert Cecil, whose family still own the Manor of Cranborne. It was not until 1828 that the Chase Rights were abolished, having become more and more of an anachronism. It is said with truth that a man had to stand by and watch a deer eat his corn, knowing that someone else had the right to kill the same deer and eat it. In 1791 the Noblemen of Cranborne Chase had proposed the disfranchisement of the Chase, as their property and the public were being injured by the "Chase Rights". The Chase, they said, was

"a den of temptation, vice and immorality, the parishes were nests for deer stealers 'bred to it by their parents' and a harbour for smugglers who worked with the deer stealers".

There were many Verwood poachers, the unlucky or unskilful of whom spent time in the cells of the Manor House at Cranborne and in later years were sent to Dorchester Gaol.

As has been seen, there is little doubt that settlement in the Verwood area began along the banks of the River Crane which offered immediate watering for stock bounded by alluvial soil for cultivation and pasture. Potterne Farm is mentioned in documents as early as the 13th Century, Romford Mill and Manor Farm, then known as Cray's Manor, are well documented in the 1600s.

There had been a chapel in the grounds of Manor Farm, a field still being called "Chapel Hays" in a map of 1847. It was a Chapel of Ease of the important monastic foundation at Cranborne but was in ruins by 1666. Again, in the same garden previously mentioned at Three Legged Cross, stones with ecclesiastical carvings have been found which may have come from this chapel or from the other nearby abbey at Horton. Since it was common practice to take material from obsolete buildings to help with new ones, the remains of the chapel, if it were stone built, are very likely scattered over the Verwood area.

It seems likely that most of the farms close to the Crane, where the most fertile land lies, are on very ancient sites indeed. Anomalies are Burrows and Eastworth Farms which stand well apart from the Crane but are also on ancient sites. Romford Mill, the last surviving watermill serving Verwood, just inside Edmondsham parish, though rebuilt in the 18th Century, is recorded in documents of the early 17th Century as for a short time being a fulling mill, processing cloth rather than its more usual function of foodstuffs. Before it ceased active production in the early part of the twentieth century, it was a 'gristing' mill, grinding animal feed.

For the most part, over the years, Verwood "slept", the tenor of day to day life being untroubled by outside events, but in 1685 politics and religion caught up with the area when after the Catholic James II had crushed the Protestant Monmouth Rebellion, the Duke of Monmouth was captured under an ash tree on Horton Heath on July 8th after fleeing from the battle of Sedgemoor in Somerset.

Hutchins tells us that

> *"the Duke went onto the Island, as it is called, a cluster of small farms in the middle of the heath, and there concealed himself in a deep ditch under an ash tree. When the pursuers came up, a woman living in a neighbouring cot gave information of his being somewhere in the island, which was immediately surrounded by soldiers, who passed the night there and threatened to fire the neighbouring cots. As they were going away next morning, one of them espied the brown skirt of the Duke's coat and seized him. The soldier no sooner knew him than he burst into tears and reproached himself for the unhappy discovery. The family of the woman who first gave the information are said to have fallen into decay and never thrived afterwards. Farmer Kerley's grandmother who died in the early part of the last century (18th), saw him and described him as a black, genteel, tall man, with a dejected countenance."*

Monmouth was taken to Holt Lodge, then Ringwood and executed on Tower Hill on July 15th less than a month after landing. He had a lot of support from the lower classes and one wonders how the people of Verwood felt. His memory lives on in Verwood in the Duke's Court flats and the Monmouth Ash public house whilst a replacement ash tree marks the spot where he was captured on Horton Heath though the site is now in private hands. The merciless revenge exacted on the rebels and their supporters, notably through the notorious "Hanging Judge" Jeffries at the "Bloody Assizes", still reverberates around the south west of England over 300 years later.

THE EIGHTEENTH CENTURY AND THE SMUGGLERS

The Turnpike Road through Three Legged Cross with the old Traveller's Rest Inn

The eighteenth century brought with it the building of many turnpike roads. In 1756 there were several from Poole Gate into Cranborne Chase and in 1759 two more were established, one of which ran from Ringwood through Woolsbridge, Three Legged Cross and Horton. These roads were paid for by the tolls collected from travellers and the importance of

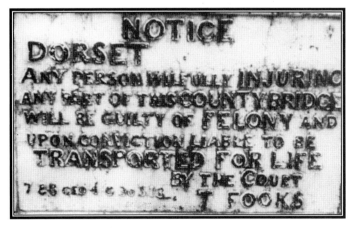

maintaining them and their fabric is reflected in the signs found on many Dorset bridges warning that the penalty for damage was transportation for life. Great anger and temptation was no doubt felt by those who had been used to traversing these former countryside trackways without charge.

1760 found Cranborne on the high road from London to the west. These roads brought more people to the area. The smugglers certainly used them, the Chase woods, which were much more plentiful at that time, being a good refuge when conveying their contraband from the coast to inland destinations.

Telegraph Hill to the north of Verwood was a landmark in Napoleonic times. It was one of a line of telegraph posts strung out across the country from London to Plymouth. This system of semaphore could flash a message from Devon to London and carry a reply within minutes. The news of Nelson's Trafalgar travelled by this means so perhaps Verwood was celebrating the victory, tempered by its sad news, fractionally before London.

THE EIGHTEENTH CENTURY AND THE SMUGGLERS

The imposition of excise duties during the wars with France encouraged the smugglers to defraud the government of revenue. Smuggling had been confined to Kent and Sussex, but when the Coast Blockade was set up in that area on land and sea, smuggling became risky and profits were lost. The smugglers then moved along to the coasts of Hampshire and Dorset and many local people became involved in the trade. The broken coasts of these counties gave many opportunities for the smugglers to land.

One of the four main routes inland through Dorset lay from Christchurch and Boscombe via Ringwood and Verwood (Burrows Lane) to Cranborne. Isaac Gulliver, the well known local smuggler, is also said to have brought his goods up through West Moors and Three Legged Cross. As the routes from Christchurch, Boscombe and Canford converged on Cranborne, great efforts were made in this area to put an end to the illicit traffic. At Cranborne and Verwood, Excise Officers and Dragoons were quartered and many encounters took place.

On March 9th 1779 the Excise Officer at Cranborne received information of a train of twenty horses in the vicinity and duly despatched his dragoons to intercept them. The smugglers were overcome easily, but while returning to Cranborne with the captured contraband, the dragoons were countered by fifty smugglers, losing all their horses. The dragoons reached Cranborne with many wounded and two dead. Reinforcement dragoons were sent from Wimborne Minster and two smugglers were captured. One died of his wounds and the other was hung in chains at Eastworth.

Eastworth Farmhouse, also the "Heathpoult Inn" in the 18th and 19th centuries

The present Eastworth Farmhouse, then also the "Heathpoult Inn", dates from around this period and it is believed that contraband was concealed beneath the floorboards in times of need. The small attic window under each eave would have provided a good lookout point.

There were doubtless many willing local participants in the trade in times when a night's work, albeit risky, could earn more than a week's wage but only one Verwood smuggler is known by name. He was a desperate character known as "Dan of Verwood", whom we now know to have been Daniel Sims, one of the ten children of William Sims the then miller at Romford and who seems to have attained the status of folk hero in the village.

This status was, no doubt, considerably enhanced by his possession of a "beautiful white horse which could fight four or five men".

On one occasion when Dan was "industriously cutting turves on the Common" the Cranborne Exciseman, on information received, searched Dan's house which stood to the rear of where the Methodist Church and Town Council Office now are and found, secreted in an underground cell, eleven kegs of liquor which he then carried off to his house in Cranborne. On being told of this, Dan, unperturbed, rode straight to Cranborne, went into the Fleur de Lys and sat quietly down in the chimney corner with his pipe and glass until inevitably someone came bounding in with the news.

Having ascertained where the kegs were lodged, Dan then rode south and recruited some of his friends or business partners who at midnight congregated with their horses and carts at the crossroads just south of Cranborne, called "Deadmans", from a legendary belief that a suicide is buried there. A local man was then sent ahead to mark the Exciseman's house with chalk so that no mistake should be made in the darkness.

Dan and his band followed, one beating in the door with a sledge hammer whilst another stood in the street with a horse pistol, threatening to blow out the brains of the Exciseman or of any other person who offered to resist them. When the "goods" were secured, they loaded their carts and with one outrider in front, armed, and another in the rear they galloped away. The incident invited no further repercussion from the Excise Service but provided a prime object for gossip in the local Public Houses.

Dan was never captured and survived until 1826 when he met an untimely end at the age of 66, being dragged in his stirrup by his horse. He was buried in Cranborne Churchyard, there being no burial place in Verwood until 1829. He was survived by his unmarried son Daniel, a wheelwright, who lived on in the house with his widowed sister Mary Richardson. When the house was sold, 50 or 60 guns were found in it, relics of old Dan's trade.

As a footnote to the above, in 1879 Daniel Sims junior by his Will established a charity under which best bread was to be distributed to the inhabitants of Verwood on 21st December each year St. Thomas, whose feast day this officially was, then being dispensed with by most of the local populace who rechristened it "Dan's Day".

During the 18th Century, substantial building and rebuilding was carried out on the more important houses and farms in the neighbourhood. Apart from these, there are several cob cottages, the homes of the ordinary villagers, built from earlier times up to the 20th Century. It would be interesting to know which of them is the oldest but as methods of construction remained the same and title deeds are not forthcoming on this point, recording merely the first change of ownership, not the original foundation, this would be hard to prove.

So Verwood entered the phase of what we would term the beginning of modern life.

THE NINETEENTH CENTURY ONWARDS

A COMPOSITE 19TH CENTURY VERWOOD SCENE
Showing the Smallholders, Pottery, Besoms and the newly installed Railway
As the underlying heathland rises to Cranborne Chase

In post medieval times, landowners in this area included the Earl of Pembroke, Lord Rivers, the Lords of Salisbury, Shaftesbury and Normanton, Lady Bingham, the Brounker and Fryer families. The returns of owners of land of 1871 shows that none of the large landowners lived in Verwood. The first to do so was one of the Fryer family, by that time Lords of the Manor of Verwood, who built the Manor House in the early 1890s. It was to be a brief sojourn though well remembered for the novel excitement of a "Big House" – carriages, gentry coming and going, large landscaped gardens and a resident Squire, but the family had left by 1920 less than thirty years later.

A curiosity is that Horatio Nelson owned land in Verwood for a time as is still shown in the deeds of some local houses. This was the 3rd Earl (1823-1913), great-nephew and namesake of the famous admiral. He lived at Trafalgar House near Downton, Wiltshire and was married to Lady Mary Jane Diana Agar, daughter of the 2nd Earl of Normanton of Somerley House. Admiral Horatio Nelson's sister Catherine had also lived nearby with her husband George Matcham from 1790 to 1806, their former estate still bearing the family name "Matchams".

Lady Bingham, remembered in some street names, was the widow of General Sir George Ridout Bingham, a hero of the Napoleonic Wars who had inherited Potterne Farm through his mother's family, the Ridouts of Deans Leaze near Witchampton.

A stone which used to stand near the present Ferrett Green marked the meeting place of three great estates, Shaftesbury to the west, Normanton to the north and east with Fryer to the south. Other estate boundary stones have been found including one on a pathway off Church Hill, at Verwood Farm and north of Ringwood Road.

THE NINETEENTH CENTURY ONWARDS

The more profitable farms, with the exception of one at Woolsbridge in the private ownership of the Witt family, belonged to large estates such as these and were managed or tenanted on their behalf. The rest of the land, much on sandy Bagshot Beds, was not considered worth cultivating and as such was never enclosed. Shrewder families seem to have been able to acquire small parcels of land from Estate Ownership on which they settled themselves or rented out to other villagers. Especially at Three Legged Cross these parcels of land were turned into family smallholdings.

From time immemorial, the Crane Valley and other farms would have needed ancillary workers such as labourers, blacksmiths, carpenters and thatchers. The population steadily grew but a large influx took place in the 1800s. The population of 327 in 1818 had more than doubled by the time of the 1841 census to 683 and rose in the next ten years to 919. This population was scattered over a wide area including most of Three Legged Cross which has always been part of Verwood for parochial and local government purposes.

Immigration into Verwood during the late eighteenth and nineteenth centuries perhaps began initially when Enclosure Acts in other neighbouring villages excluded some of their native population. Those with no land rights would have had to leave if they could not find employment in order to support themselves, whilst pottery making was considered an unsocial trade; clay pits were dug but not filled in to the hazard of the population and fuel for firing taken from any available source whether by right or not. The general population was also rising and in lean times the traditional agricultural villages would not have been able to offer support to all. Verwood, with its large uncultivated tracts of heathland and nearby sources of clay, proved a haven for both the potters and the generally unemployed.

A typical Verwood thatched cob house
Mrs. Charlotte Haskell outside Ghillie Cottage, Ebblake

The newcomers and newly-married couples carved a piece out of the common, just large enough for them to work themselves, which they gradually improved with back-breaking toil between their employment and other daily tasks, until they could grow vegetables and as fortunes progressed keep a pig and some chickens and perhaps a dairy cow.

THE NINETEENTH CENTURY ONWARDS

The cottages were simple two up two down mudwall (cob) constructions, the cheapest and most readily available building material.   The clay or "mud" as it was termed was dug from adjoining land or a suitable patch on the common.   Ferrett Green in the centre of Verwood was once a large mud pit for the Crossroads Pottery.   The clay was mixed with dung, horsehair, heather and other binding materials then "reared" between two long boards to a height of about two feet all round.   When the first rearing was dry, a second would be placed on top, allowing for windows and doors.   This progressed to the roof which was thatched with local straw.   In this way a cottage could be built with minimum to no outlay.   The standard pattern, unvaried over the years was a central throughway with a room each side both up and down.   A hearth and chimney was usually only built at one end only to service the kitchen living area and "master bedroom".   Water supply was from the nearest well and the privy sited at the bottom of the garden.

Verwood from Black Hill showing a random building pattern of houses surrounded by fields and gardens

The landowners allowed this indiscriminate settlement to happen, considering the land to be of little practical use to themselves, indeed at times members of the Fryer family were most generous in donation of land for both public and private use and any charges were small. However, it is said that in other cases it was a very different story, the incoming families being simple folk who believed that they would be able to settle at no expense beyond the building of their cottage but that the bailiff would soon arrive to see that rent was paid or a token amount paid to the landowner in recognition of his freehold rights. Leases were often taken on the cottages usually on a lifehold basis involving three named lives. These were not necessarily on the lives of the people who could be thought to succeed to the lease but formed a sort of lottery when any three persons could be named and the lease expired when the last of them died. It would have been a brave gamble to name a young child who might live to the age of ninety but even more likely die before maturity.

The settlement pattern of 1847 shows a small nucleus around Church Hill and Dewlands Common with ribbon development along Cranborne to Ringwood Road, now Station and Ringwood Roads, and the Horton to Ringwood Road through Three Legged Cross. Apart from this there was much encroachment on the commons and the beginning of present day Verwood roads started to form.

The legacy of this indiscriminate building could be seen quite clearly just a few years ago with long strips of spread out houses each in its own large garden interspersed by fields and woods but is today perhaps only evident in the rather peculiar shape of some of Verwood's roads. The bends in Newtown Road skirted different pieces of property as did those at Crab Orchard although both have been graded in recent years to reduce their former sharp zig-zag lines. Even the main roads were unsurfaced until the late 1920s, dusty in summer, muddy in winter and treacherously potholed throughout.

The passage of traction engines on roads not designed for them created concern similar to that caused by juggernaut lorries today. In 1903 Wimborne and Cranborne Rural District Council tried to obtain compensation from a Cranborne haulier for the damage to roads between Wyke Bottom, through St. Giles and Verwood to the County boundary at Ebblake on his way to Ringwood. The Clerk to Ringwood R.D.C., however, advised the man that since he was carrying flint and chalk for (Hampshire) road repairs he should be exempt from liability for the damage he had caused!

In the end a figure was agreed and the money obtained "after considerable pressure" by the District Surveyor. Such incidents were not uncommon and the Council refused to make any repairs to roads for which they disclaimed responsibility as once they had done so it would become a precedent.

At Romford bridge, a traction engine stops to draw water whilst a "higgler"
looses his horse to drink before taking his cart across the ford.
The cart wheels also needed to be in water from time to time to "plim them up".

As the Surveyor pointed out, there were hundreds of miles of droves in his area and to repair one would have laid the Council open to repair all. The legacy is the now dwindling number of Verwood roads which still have a rough surface, a familiar sight only a few years ago.

Even those acknowledged by the R.D.C. fared little better at times. In 1905 Rev. H. Drake, the curate, sent a letter urging Council repairs as "the three main roads out of Verwood were not in even a fairly passable condition for many days together at any season of the year". However the Vice Chairman and several Councillors familiar with the roads complained of by Mr. Drake entirely supported the Surveyor in his contention "that the condition of these roads was quite satisfactory and in fact had never been better".

The road to Horton and the south via Margards Lane, now scarcely more than a track, was more important than the one to Three Legged Cross which meandered across the common, forded the Crane near Manor Farm and meandered back out onto the commons again. The present stretch between Three Legged Cross and Potterne was described as a "new road" in 1903. At one time when there were three gates through Manor Farm land across the road between Verwood and Three Legged Cross, an awkward farmer took great delight in locking the middle thus causing maximum annoyance to travellers from either end.

Until bridges were built, many of the approaches into Verwood and Three Legged Cross required a ford and for the remaining years of horse drawn transport and stock droving the fords were kept alongside the new bridges. Even when in later years the road between Verwood and Three Legged Cross was rerouted, it crossed through a ford at Potterne. In the early twentieth century the Vicar, Rev. Claud Brown, was instrumental in getting the bridge built there after his carriage, bearing an important visitor, had overturned in the ford.

In addition many paths, droves and bridleways crisscrossed the landscape as the shortest means of reaching one place from another. It is only in very recent years that some of the previously minor roads have been made up but some which still remain in their original condition serve to remind us of the prevailing conditions of former days. The old pattern of Verwood is now, of course, completely superimposed by the new and though many cob cottages remain, many more have been demolished and several large gardens, fields and woods sold for building land in the face of high density development.

Some of the villagers had trades such as blacksmiths, carpenters, shoemakers, thatchers and especially at Three Legged Cross and Crab Orchard the more enterprising newcomers set themselves up as basket and broom or "besom" makers. In early twentieth century Directories practically the entire Dorset workforce in this trade lived in Verwood and Three Legged Cross. Pottery making was established in the northern half of the area employing a few families and thus sprinkling the predominately agricultural environment with light industry. This in turn enabled others to become pottery dealers or "higglers", taking Verwood goods for sale over a wide area.

The overwhelming majority of adult men, however, described themselves as Agricultural Labourers, an uncertain profession at the best of times, dependent on weather, seasons, foreign imports and their own health.

In the early 1830s England was in a state of agricultural unrest. Swing riots, Chartist riots, Reform Bills, Corn Laws brought enraged mobs pounding at landowners' doors within not many miles of Verwood. In 1830 a guard was kept at Cranborne Manor House from November 24th to December 7th consisting of sixteen men and horses relieved daily. On 24th November the mob had come to Boveridge just to the north.

THE NINETEENTH CENTURY ONWARDS

More peaceably, in Tolpuddle, the labourers had attempted to improve their lot by negotiation but were transported to Australia in 1834, having been convicted on a technicality. Dorset landowners still held the fear of mass revolution as had been experienced just over the Channel in France only a generation previously. The story is told more fully in numerous publications but the connection with Verwood is less widely known.

Two of the six "Martyrs" were Thomas Standfield, aged 44, and his 21 year old son John. Thomas was the eldest surviving child of about nine born to Robert and Elizabeth (Betty Baker) Standfield, from a long established Tolpuddle family which had had a substantial carpentry business, farming interests and presided at the local inn. Thomas had additional emotional ties to Tolpuddle in that in 1812 at the age of 22 he had married Diana Loveless, sister of the future Martyr's leader, George and another member James. By the time of the transportation they had seven children ranging in age between 21 and 5.

THE STANDFIELD GRAVES IN VERWOOD CHURCHYARD
The upright stones commemorate Robert & Elizabeth (Betty), the parents of Thomas "the Martyr";
Their son Robert with his wife Arabella; Their grandson Ernest Richard son of Richard and Ann.
The table tomb is the burial place of their son William of Verwood Farm and his wife Jane.

Thomas' sister Elizabeth married farmer Hezekiah Talbot of Holton, Wareham in 1820 but somewhere between then and 1832 all connection of the rest of the family with West Dorset ceased. Thomas and Betty with five younger unmarried children Robert, William, James Baker, Richard and Charity left the area to settle in completely different farming country. Certainly they were in Verwood by 1832 when Robert senior was buried in Verwood Churchyard and Charity married John Keeping a farmer at Mannington near Three Legged Cross. In 1841 Robert junior was living at East Farm, Romford just inside the boundaries of Edmondsham parish whilst William, as Head of Household, was at Verwood Farm, off Margards Lane, with James, Richard and their widowed mother. James later married and farmed at Mannington whilst Richard first assisted his brother William, then moved to a farm on Eastworth Road, the buildings of which have long since disappeared. He briefly lived at Eling, near Totton, Southampton before returning to Verwood once more.

In stark contrast to Thomas' humble station in life as an agricultural labourer supporting his family on a few meagre shillings a week at Tolpuddle, the Standfields in Verwood were thought of as "well-to-do" and one of Verwood's major farming families.

William leased Verwood Farm from Lord Shaftesbury where he managed a very large acreage extending into Horton parish and encompassing Bridge Farm in Horton Way. He was obviously a successful farmer, no doubt bred to the role by his father and forebears, and adapted to the very different soil conditions. He died in 1891 aged 91, his much younger wife Jane having long predeceased him. Two sons, Albert and Frank, followed him at the farm whilst another, Tom Richard, became one of the first proprietors of steam thrashing machines in the area. John became a Baker, Grocer and Innkeeper at the New Inn on Church Hill, Verwood before acting as a Farm Manager in Berkshire. William James held nearby Woodlands Manor Farm in 1871, moved to farm in Clarendon, Wiltshire by 1881 but by 1891 had returned to Lower Farm, now West Farm, Romford. Here, his small daughter Amy carved her name with her mother's diamond ring on a pane of glass in one of the bedrooms.

The younger children of both the martyrs and those who remained at home were never told of the court case and transportation. In the same way as those whose ancestors were transported for criminal reasons, a falsified picture or veil of secrecy was drawn over their origins. It is only from the latter quarter of the twentieth century that such ancestors were regarded as to be prized instead of to be ashamed of.

However the living standards of Verwood's labourers were more akin to those of Thomas, who had remained in his native village, and the lesson of the transportation would not have been lost on them. Agriculture fluctuated and at times was very low; wheat could be unloaded at Weymouth for less than the cost of growing it locally. The Industrial Revolution sent scores of starving labourers flocking to the towns in search of any employment. Perhaps Verwood was saved from the worst excesses in most cases because each cottage had land attached to supplement the diet and therefore the very fact that it was designated poor agricultural soil was to prove the salvation of its inhabitants who could at least eke out an existence in bad times.

A Verwood "Higgler", cart loaded with pots and brooms

Money could also be made by the sale of excess and specially grown produce to the growing town of Bournemouth as well as at local markets such as Ringwood and Wimborne which provided an opportunity to buy, sell and exchange goods over a wider area. Farmers and smallholders also drove their cattle to the regional stock sales at Wimborne market.

THE NINETEENTH CENTURY ONWARDS

One higgler made the journey to Bournemouth by horse and wagon every Saturday until 1952. Others took earthenware and besom brooms to such places as Mere, Portland, Salisbury and Basingstoke.

The women bore their part by knitting gloves, a very important secondary Verwood industry. Boys too had to take what casual employment they could find as their contribution to the family's weekly earnings was more important, when it could be obtained, than their education.

These enterprises, however hardly won, did manage to keep the Verwood population alive. Certainly most typical Dorset villages show a decline in population over the century from which they never recovered and Verwood is unusual, if not unique, in maintaining and even increasing population during these difficult times. That is not to say that no-one moved, but the traffic was not all one way.

But it was a very hand to mouth life and many Verwood fathers were driven to poaching or stealing corn to supplement the family pot. Destitute families were obliged to enter the designated Union Workhouse after 1834 when the Poor Law had changed provision from the more benign but haphazard awards by the Churchwardens from amounts raised locally to a centralized system where conditions were made such that were work available it was preferable to the harsh regime.

Verwood became part of the Wimborne and Cranborne Union for these purposes, the institution being sited in Wimborne, a town too far distant for most of the inhabitants to have visited in their lives. In one of the grimmest of those grim establishments several Verwood people, the old, widows, orphaned children, those to whom work was unavailable, occasionally feckless families and unmarried mothers were incarcerated, several of the elderly dying within its walls. One Verwood woman, Ann North, gave as good as she got by breaking the workhouse windows on one occasion after her husband had abandoned the family yet again.  Eventually the family was given outdoor relief which presumably the Guardians felt was preferable to having such an intractable inmate.

Many of the villagers, however, led good plain lives and were able through toil and circumstance to keep their families in the basic necessities of life. Religion and education played an important part in fostering a sense of self worth and self discipline, especially from the nineteenth century onwards. The Anglican, Methodist and Independent congregations each had a small chapel built in Verwood in the early 19th century, the Anglican incorporating a small burial ground which alleviated the necessity of using the parish ground in Cranborne to where the bier had formerly to be carried or pushed. Baptisms could also then take place locally. Three Legged Cross had similar chapels but without a burial ground.

Increased mechanisation brought other changes to Verwood, the most important being the coming of the railway in 1866. The day excursions which could be made to places that before had been beyond the reach of most Verwood folk brought a pleasure to add to those few simple ones which they already enjoyed as well as increasing the prospect of business and employment. The station became a focal point and with its comings and goings must have provided excitement for all.

THE NINETEENTH CENTURY ONWARDS

By 1861 Verwood had a Police Constable who lived in Somerly Cottage set well back from the road on the western border of the present parish near Romford. It was said to be originally sited there so that the parish constable could meet and escort on their rounds the collectors of tithes for the Vicar of Cranborne. This was a highly unpopular tax with those who did not conform to the Established Church. In later years the Police House was situated in Ringwood Road but this service to Verwood was eventually lost in 1969. It has only been re-established in 1994 at a purpose built complex off Station Road.

The New Inn, Margard's Lane. Drawn from a reconstruction by Mr Aubrey Barrow

By 1859 George Haskell, a Grocer and Baker, was acting as Parish Clerk and Postmaster; by 1865 the latter duty had passed to a lady, Miss Norman and by 1881 to Charles Hayter, landlord of the New Inn on Church Hill at the top of Margards Lane. By 1895 the Post Office was established in Trickett's Cottage on Manor Road and from that year the sub-postmaster, John Trickett, was allowed to deal in Money Orders. Before that villagers would have had to go outside should they have need for one. For many years telegrams continued to be dealt with at the railway station which had a telegraph. This telegraph proved invaluable to one Boy Scout, Sidney Trickett, who on an occasion when the office was unattended took down an incoming Morse message and was rewarded for his enterprise with a job on the railway. The Post Office moved to Penarth, also in Manor Road, to Vicarage Road, to Ringwood Road and has since returned to Manor Road once more. It seems that telephones did not arrive in Verwood until the second decade of the twentieth century when the Post Office number was Verwood 1 and the Station Verwood 2.

In 1895 it was also recorded that "there is a conveyance from Verwood Station to the Victoria (now with its original name of the Sheaf of Arrows) in Cranborne twice daily", though there must have been some such system of regular carrier transport for both people and goods from the earliest days of the railway. Several tradesmen offered a horse and trap "taxi" service, one of the best remembered in later years being Mr. Franklin of the New Inn.

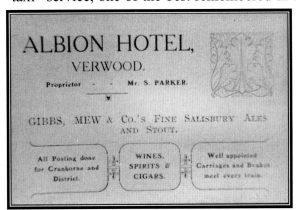

A carriage service was also provided by the Albion Hotel and a resident of Woodlands vividly remembers that on a still night the porters' shouts of "Verwood", the slamming of train doors, followed by the clip-clopping of the horse's hooves as the proprietor's young son took travellers back to outlying villages, carried clearly over the countryside. Mr. Vince Parker, a son of the Albion Licensee Samuel, took early advantage of motor cars by starting his own taxi service.

PARISH STATUS AND
THE TWENTIETH CENTURY

By 1886 Verwood had established its corporate identity and as the ecclesiastical parish of Cranborne had become too large and unwieldy Verwood and Alderholt were taken from it to form two new parishes. Until 1922 Verwood also included West Moors which had been taken from the parish of West Parley. The old Anglican chapel on Church Hill had had a brick chancel added in 1870 but extensive building work was carried out to fit it for its new status as the Parish Church.

The Local Government Act of 1894 decreed that all villages of 300 or more inhabitants had to have a Parish Council. Verwood became a Civil Parish on 5th March 1894 with the first election held the following 17th December. It was part of Wimborne and Cranborne Rural District Council, following the pattern of the Union made under the Poor Law Act of 1834.

The twentieth century dawned with no particularly significant effect on the people of Verwood. They were better educated than their forebears but work in general followed the same patterns. Much of the land was still in the hands of the large estates which led to disputes as to right of lease and ownership.

The "Verwood Fire Ruins"

Former home of Joseph Trickett, his wife Fanny, née Haskell, and their nine surviving children.

In 1906 when the unmarried Squire William Rolles Fryer died, his childless brother Henry Charles, then already aged 75, inherited the Manor and his land in Verwood. Henry, twice married, had lived for a considerable number of years in the Aberystwyth area of Wales where he had been a farmer and a Clerk of the Peace for Cardigan. It would not be unexpected then if his primary interests lay outside Verwood. He died in 1921 in Southbourne so evidently returned to the broad area of his roots in Lytchett Minster. The only brother with descendants, Frederick Rolles Fryer, had been a long time resident of Australia which has caused difficulties in later years with reference to the legality of bequests and conditions laid thereon by earlier members of the family.

However, when Henry Charles inherited, a branch of the Trickett family had a smallholding in Newtown Road around the present Claylake Drive. The new Squire laid claim to this wanting to put a man of his own in for his own profit. The Tricketts claimed that the land belonged to them and had a great deal of sympathy in this amongst the villagers.

However, they were summarily evicted but came back in the night with some likeminded friends and revenged themselves on the Squire by burning down the house and cutting every tree to about two feet from the ground. The place was "swarming with police" but it was the general opinion that, having then fled the district, they would never be caught and it is unlikely that they would have been if someone had not "opened up" in the words of an old Verwood resident.

However, when the police were informed of the relevant names, they soon rounded up the miscreants, one at least being found at the Curragh in Ireland. The ringleaders were given sentences of up to five years. It is said that this branch of the family held land at Trickett's Cross and that after their eviction some settled there and built a house, thus giving the place its name. However, this origin of the name Trickett's Cross is disputed by others and perhaps one day an interested resident there may discover the true story. The "Verwood Fire Ruins" became of sufficient interest to merit a picture postcard.

The children of St. Gabriel's Home with their carers (courtesy of Barry Cuff)

A newcomer to Verwood in 1901 was Miss Violet Tennyson, a niece of the poet, who founded St. Gabriel's Home for orphaned girls in Ringwood Road. Correspondence reveals Miss Tennyson as a deeply caring lady with a continued interest in the welfare of her charges. Later Father Hanson, a retired priest, lived there and during the 1926 General Strike put a wireless on the windowsill so that villagers could hear the latest news. The house was later occupied by Letchers, Solicitors but has now reverted to its original purpose, this time for adults in need of residential care.

The population in 1901 was 1007 in the civil and 1291 in the ecclesiastical parish. A brick industry had begun in the middle of the previous century with sites at Black Hill and the station. Roofing tiles were made at a kiln set back on the northern side of the Cranborne road near, Romford. To begin with these bricks were hand made by a few local families but, as trade grew with the coming of the railway, these businesses expanded and brick kilns and chimneys were built. The Manor Brickworks at Black Hill, owned by Squire Fryer, was developed in this way about 1914. The Verwood and Gotham Brick and Tile Company owned the yard by the Station and eventually took over one to the north previously owned by the Hopkins family. Both were owned by Southern United Brick Company before closure.

Some of the more prestigious buildings in the locality, including Bournemouth Pavilion, were made from Verwood brick. There was also, until about 1909, a brickyard at Ebblake manufacturing white bricks from a seam of local clay. These bricks were used for decoration and many examples can be seen in the village today as well as further afield. With the smoke billowing from their chimneys and the fiery glow from the potters' kilns, Verwood must have presented an unusually industrial face in the midst of a very rural environment.

Associated with the Black Hill brickworks was a village band, preferential employment being given to those who could play an instrument. Verwood has a long tradition of band playing and one bandmaster, Fred Fry, was said to be able to play any instrument you gave him. Being a potter, he made himself a set of perfectly tuned flower pots on which he was able to play any hymn or tune.

Verwood did not have its own doctor until 1921 when Dr. Girling held his surgery at the Restynge House. Before that, if the case was serious enough, the doctor rode over on horseback from Cranborne. One assumes, therefore, that someone had to walk or ride there to fetch him. The doctor did not appear to be on the telephone at home until the 1930s, there being little point, one assumes, if the majority of his patients did not have access to one or perhaps he foresaw his off duty hours being disturbed if one were installed.

The First World War came and went, leaving a gash in the hearts of those who knew and loved the young men from Verwood who died. A wooden memorial cross was erected in the churchyard to their memory after the war ended but some years later it blew down in a storm and was replaced by the present one of Portland Stone. Fortunately the figure of Christ was saved and attached to the new memorial. Later, of course, were added the names of those who died in the Second World War and Malayan Emergency.

The old wooden War Memorial in St. Michael & All Angels Churchyard

The Recreation Ground was purchased by public subscription as a memorial to those lost during World War I, with a tree planted for every man who fell. A pavilion was given by ex-servicemen in memory of their fallen comrades. In more recent years a commemorative plaque has been placed on the gates of the Recreation Ground and a memorial stone is sited on Ferrett Green.

Verwood C.E. School Gardening Class 9th April 1919 with teacher, Mr. Summers, the Vicar's Gardener.
The Class photo on Page 62 was also taken on the same date when a photographer attended for this purpose
Hence the boys are wearing their "best" clothes minus jackets

One side effect of the First World War was to reintroduce agriculture into the schools' curriculum. Previously these country children had had a purely academic education, not fitting them at all, as some critics pointed out, for what life held in store for them. Now the gardening classes which had recently begun were intensified and each school set aside land where the boys were instructed in basic cultivation.

Another off-shoot of the conflict was the development of the village sawmills. The Thorne family of Romford mill had already diversified into steam threshing and timber but Robert Thorne also foresaw the need for trench props during the fighting in France and so began a thriving business in an area of woodlands. He bought two traction engines, one being called "King of the Forest", and these could take three truckloads of bricks daily to Blandford Army Camp as well as provide power for threshing and sawing. The threshing trade has come to an end with the advent of the Combine Harvester but the sawmill, which was moved to Dewlands Road after the war, only ceased production in 1998, the land now developed as Old Sawmill Close. Until at least 1984 one hurdle maker remained with the firm and stacks of hurdles could be seen awaiting delivery. Most of these were then for ornamental purposes rather than their original function of lambing pens.

In the 1920s and 30s Verwood was well served by many small bakers, shops, businesses and delivery rounds. Where any deficiencies occurred arrangements could be made to overcome them. For instance Barrow Brothers who ran a bakery and shop in Ringwood Road used to collect medicines from Ringwood for customers and distribute them on their next round. By 1923 both the National Provincial and Lloyds Banks had limited opening hours in the village.

There was also an increase in social clubs and societies including a Tennis and Bowling Club, Working Men's Institute, Cricket and Football Clubs, Women's Institute and Scouts and Guides as well as other organizations attached to the various churches.

Verwood Carnival was started in 1929 by the Vicar's wife, Mrs. Jeayes, and a group of friends, to replace the annual fair held on Church Hill which had lapsed after 1925. Rev. Wilfrid Arthur Jeayes was the incumbent from 1927 until his early death in 1934 at the age of 45 after an operation in London which went wrong. As he and his wife had several children they occupied the large Victorian Vicarage which had been let since the days of Rev. Claud Brown.   Rev. Jeayes' brother Allan was a distinguished theatre and film actor, one of whose most prestigious roles was as General Faversham in the 1938 film "The Four Feathers".

The Carnival was suspended during the War Years but reinstated in 1946 and continues as an annual event on the late May Bank Holiday Monday.

The Royal float heads the first Post-World War Two Carnival procession along Ringwood Road.

Carnival Queen - Daphne Sims. Attendants facing backwards Brenda Shearing and Doris Mills. Facing forwards, left Peggy Reeks and right Jean Penny Ernie Young is driving the tractor.

A small Village Hall on the north-east corner of the Crossroads was replaced by the Memorial Hall in 1959, dedicated to the fallen of WWII, after very many years of hard work, fund raising and saving.

The Hants and Dorset Motor Services acquired the operator's licence and vehicles of E. H. Saunders' 'Verwood Motor Service' in January 1937. It was the last pre-war addition to the Bournemouth depot.

At this time the traditional Verwood pottery industry was suffering its final decline. The Cross Roads Pottery, the last to operate, managed to survive the War Years though in later times producing mainly fancy goods but that enterprise too closed in 1952. Two of the last great master potters working there were Meshech Sims and Herbert Bailey. There is now only one surviving pottery mound in the Verwood area, which is being kept by the present owner as an example of the many that used to dot the landscape. Ironically, Verwood Pottery is now enjoying a boom and has become a collector's item.   The cob workshed of the Crossroads Pottery was saved by the efforts of Verwood Museum Trust and has now re-opened with modern additions as Verwood Heathland Heritage Centre.

During the 1930s more building work began to shape the face of Verwood. Bungalows and houses were built by Percy Bailey along Ringwood and Manor Roads and family houses along Station and Manor Roads by Fred Sims. Fred Sims was born to a pottery family in the cottage in Newtown Road later owned by Jessie Matthews, the vivacious musical comedy star, now only remembered by the older generation.

PARISH STATUS AND THE TWENTIETH CENTURY

As the potteries failed, some employees had sought work in the brickyards but soon these too were to be gone forever. They had suffered a decline during the First World War when the young men of the village had been called up but the Second World War brought final closure as the industry depended on the kilns being continuously fired which was not possible under the blackout regulations. Also the clay which had been sliced from the top of Black Hill had run out and although there was talk of taking more from the opposite side of the road, land also owned by the brickworks, now Strathmore and Sherwood Drives, nothing came of it and the industry died.

Verwood suffered several bombing raids and on one occasion the heath was set alight with thick smoke palling the area. There was one particularly terrifying night, 23rd/24th April 1944, when bombs were falling continuously, but fortuitously only one human casualty, a 15 year old boy, Max Barrett, killed when a bomb dropped into the bedroom of his house in Hillside Road. His brother sharing the room had a miraculous escape. The Stephen's Castle area was used for observation and training with a searchlight operated by the Royal Observer Corps.

Again the village children were pressed into service, collecting amazing amounts of nettles, rosehips, broom tips, foxglove seeds, conkers, blackberries, salvage etc, to help with the War Effort. Troops both British and American were stationed in the village, there was an active Home Guard and the W.I., Red Cross and St. John's Ambulance found useful roles to play. Again Verwood's independent spirit showed when the A.R.P. Committee refused to accept two second hand trailer ambulances that Wimborne had bought by mistake and continually wrote demanding that their supplies should be sent forthwith.

Innovations into Verwood life during these middle years of the century were the first piped water, gas and electricity.

The first water systems were by private enterprise when Sidney Palmer led water to the western end of the village from a reservoir near Stephens Castle in the late 1920s. Job Brewer adapted an old pool for the same purpose at Noon Hill and Fred Sims used an underground source in Springfield Road to his houses in Manor Road. By 1939 Wimborne and Cranborne Rural District Council were supplying the district and sank two boreholes at Stanbridge near the Horton Inn to supply Verwood with pure water. Even so in 1944 half the houses in the village had no piped water supply. In 1959 the service was taken over and increased by the Bournemouth and District Water Company (Now Bournemouth and West Hampshire Water) who still supply the area today. Gas mains were laid into Three Legged Cross from West Moors in the mid 1930s by The Bournemouth and District Gas and Water Company, one of the first connections being The Travellers Rest (now The Woodcutters) and subsequently progressed up the Verwood Road to the village itself. The Company, founded in 1863, had been supplying both commodities until 1949 when gas was nationalised. Gas holding tanks were situated next to the Toc H hut on the site of the present band hall. Electricity followed shortly after, introduced by the "Wessex Electric Company". This Company erected overhead lines on wooden poles along main streets and potential customers were invited to apply for supply, usually in conjunction with wiring inside the property. Though welcomed by some, many people would naturally be cautious about both the expense and necessity. At all events, it was not installed in the Council School, housed in the present

library, until 1946 after the Head had been begging the managers for permission to install it, even offering to cover the cost from his own pocket in anticipation of their grant. At times, he reported, it was so dark in the building that he was unable to see the children across the room. When the electricity was switched on it was recorded in the school log book that "a great cheer went up".

Mains drainage was another service slow to cover this scattered community. Even in 1965, 625 houses in the village, including those along main roads, had either septic tanks or cesspools while 83 had only earth closets. It was not until 1970 that a comprehensive sewage system was installed.

Verwood Station looking very forlorn after its closure in 1965

The change which brought most sadness to the people of Verwood was the closure of the railway line under the Beeching axe. Passenger services ended in 1964 and goods the following year. The station had long been a focal point and the train used for shopping in Poole, mothers travelling with baby's pram in the Guard's van, trips to London, commercial usages and older children going to Grammar School, the boys to the Old Queen Elizabeth's at Wimborne and the girls to Parkstone, others to private schools and as weekly boarders to Weymouth Technical College. One of the boys who used to make the journey was Lionel Jeffries, the famous actor and director, whose father ran the Central Garage opposite the Recreation Ground.

In the 1960s more building development began with the estates at Owls Road and Pine View Road. Lacking first rate agricultural soil and having little visible evidence of historical value, Verwood was a natural target for the planners to create a new housing centre and so the infilling and creation of new estates began. In 1961 it was reported that

"there is a preponderance of elderly people and relatively few of family raising age compared with the national average. If projections were made on these figures to 1981 there would be an increase of only 165 persons, so increase in the long term must be through inward migration".

In 1966 the population of Verwood Parish was 3310, that of Verwood village alone 2565. At that time two thirds of the working population was still employed locally. Now the industrial estates at Ebblake and Three Legged Cross employ a proportion but many more commute to Bournemouth, Poole, Southampton, Salisbury and further afield.

During the scorching hot summers of 1975 and 1976 the surrounding heathland was plagued by outbreaks of fires. On 11th July 1976 Verwood briefly made the national news when flames swept through Ringwood Forest cutting off the village from the east.

PARISH STATUS AND THE TWENTIETH CENTURY

Inside Verwood and Three Legged Cross the building work continued with some estates lying dormant for years, others mushrooming overnight. By 1999 the estimated population was 12,330 and since that date many more houses have been built and families arrived or grown to fill them. The latest government figure in 2004 was of 13,580 – still rising.

One can understand only too well those who have lived here all their lives feeling swamped by the changes that have taken place over the last few years but fortunately Verwood and Three Legged Cross seem able to retain their village spirit and many newcomers find a warmth of welcome that delights them.

To prove that it is still a beautiful or "Fair Wood", climb up to Stephen's Castle and look down over the area where scarcely a roof can be seen. Within the fair wood, major additions in recent years have been a Town Council Chamber, formerly Lloyds Bank with a new bank in Manor Road. Safeway supermarket opened in 1982 becoming Morrison's in 2005. A Fire Station, Police Station and a replacement Doctors' surgery have been built along once rural Station Road. Verwood Church of England First School was opened in 1985 in Howe Lane to replace the original buildings on Church Hill with great excitement when it was officially declared open by Princess Margaret in July 1986. Emmanuel Middle School was built in 1990 to save the necessity of Verwood children travelling to Cranborne or West Moors whilst Trinity in 2001 added to the complement of First Schools. A Day Care Centre has opened at Baker's Farm off Station Road, joined in 2007 by "The Hub" purpose built entertainment and social centre. The Parish, Methodist and United Reformed Churches have all been extended whilst at Three Legged Cross the Evangelical Chapel and All Saints Church of England have both been completely rebuilt. The community within thrives with many clubs and activities for all ages in both the northern and southern halves of the parish.

Three Legged Cross residents show their delight at winning the "Best Village Hall" Competition in 1989
Eve Morris, George Morris, Chris East, Sid Wood, Iris Wood, Ron Campbell, Stella Turnham, Elaine Toombs

In 1987 Verwood took another step on its journey when it achieved Town status with Gordon Thorne as its first Mayor. The focus of society has changed beyond all recognition in the past two hundred years and the process continues. There will be much more to be written about the developing history of Verwood in ensuing years.

PEOPLE AND PLACES

MANOR HOUSE VERWOOD

"Squire" William Rolles Fryer, 1828-1906, was a great-grandson of the famous Dorset smuggler Isaac Gulliver on his grandmother's side. On his paternal side, he was a member of the affluent Wimborne banking family whose seat had been the Mansion House at Lytchett Minster. Like his similarly named father he owned vast tracts of land in the Verwood, Three Legged Cross, West Moors and Mannington areas as well as much more besides. Father and son were most generous in grants of land on peppercorn terms for church, school and social purposes irrespective of denomination.

William junior was a graduate of Wadham College, Oxford and had trained as a barrister. He never married and as his brothers' professions took them away from home the Lytchett property was given up and William came to reside in Verwood in the late 1880s. He built the comparatively modest Manor House which gave Manor Road its name. After his death his childless brother Henry retained the property for a few more years but it was a comparatively short lived tenure before it passed into other hands. Some of the extensive garden was later sold to develop Howard Road. The house was demolished in 1987 to make way for the Manor Court housing development.

Reverend Claud Brown, the first resident Vicar of Verwood, was also a graduate of Wadham College though some twenty-three years the Squire's junior. He arrived at about the same time and had his imposing Vicarage built on land adjoining the Squire's but separated by what became known as Vicarage Road. After Claud Brown retired in 1917 it was some years before the Vicarage was inhabited as such and it ceased to be used in this capacity at all after 1956. For a few years it housed Moorlands Bible College before being demolished for Montrose retirement flats in 1973.

3094.   The Old Vicarage, Verwood.

In 2007 the Montrose flats themselves are due to be demolished for redevelopment, residents having moved or been placed elsewhere.

The large gardens of both the Manor House and Vicarage were the scene of many festivities – Garden Parties, Fêtes, Band Concerts and such to the great enjoyment of Verwood folk.

**THE CHILDREN OF ROBERT AND ANN SIMS (NÉE FERRETT)
ON THE DAY OF THEIR MOTHER'S FUNERAL 23RD NOVEMBER 1915**

*Back far left is Fred, Potter and Builder and far right Samuel.
Between are identified Timothy, Amos, James a Policeman, and Harry
Front are daughters Rose, Jane, Kitty and Annie
Jane was crippled in an accident at the age of 3 and her voluminous skirt hides a wheelchair*

MESHECH SIMS, MASTER POTTER, WITH HIS WIFE EMILY (NÉE PALMER)
Their twins, Oscar and Owen were born in November 1908
A younger son, Ivan, was born in 1913

"THE SKEP"

This cottage which still stands in Dewlands Way is where the potter Paul Ferrett and his wife Hannah Read brought up their nine children. These included Ann born in 1843 who married Robert Sims, and Charles born 1854 who inherited the Crossroads Pottery.

Demolished in 1960, this house and workshop stood on the corner of Margards Lane and Horton Way. From the early 1890s it was home to Charles and Fanny Hibberd and family who had moved there from Bishopstone, Wiltshire.

A granddaughter of the Hibberds, born 1921, who used to enjoy childhood visits has given these reminiscences. "I don't remember the cottage having the part joined on to it with the tiled roof, maybe it was added later. The tinned roof outhouse was where granny did the washing, plucked and prepared chickens and cleaned and hung chitterlings. Grandad was disabled and walked with a crutch as one of his legs was shorter than the other. He was a Master Boot and Shoemaker and all the farm workers in the area came to him to have their boots made. The window on the left of the photo was where his shop and workshop were. His son Sidney Hibberd's farm was at the back of the cottage but it didn't have a name that I know of. We just used to call it "Uncle Sid's Farm!"

Left: Mrs. Joseph Andrews with her children Bertha Winifred, Albert Cecil and Alice Beatrice about 1887. Mrs. Andrews was formerly Leah Naomi Haskell, daughter of Joseph Haskell and Leah Colbourne. She had been a Pupil Teacher at the Church of England School in Verwood before her marriage and both daughters became teachers. Beatrice was the second wife of Ira Henning, Coal Merchant and a Verwood public figure. Right: Albert Andrews in later life examining the results of his home produced cider. Albert, who never married, became a well liked and respected Verwood craftsman. He is remembered as one of nature's true gentlemen.

The Andrews family home "Hazeldene" in Coopers Lane on the corner of Edmondsham Road, long since demolished and replaced by bungalows. Albert continued to live here using the land for his workshop and yard. Trinity First School has now been built in the field to the left of the photograph.

ADA MABEL STANDFIELD

Had a pleasing singing voice. She and her father Tom, a tenor, used to like standing together in church. Her daughter Edith Tomlinson married Ivan Sims, youngest son of Meshech and Emily.

THOMAS RICHARD "TOM" STANDFIELD

Born 1854, he was a son of William Standfield and his wife Jane Ingram of Verwood Farm. He married Rose Bailey when she was just 16 years old and he 20, having nine children. Tom was the first in the neighbourhood to have a steam threshing tackle and an extendable ladder for building ricks. His eldest son, Tom Richard, also followed in this trade and as agricultural contractors their machines were in use as far afield as Warminster. Another son, Herbert, owned and operated Road Rollers.

JAMES ANDREWS

A Verwood Farm Labourer convicted of poaching and transported to Tasmania in 1827. He settled in Melbourne becoming a prosperous, well respected citizen.

WILLIAM JAMES STANDFIELD

Eldest son of William and Jane, never shaved, retaining a virgin beard. He farmed in various locations before returning to Verwood and married three times having children by each wife.

WILLIAM PETER STICKLAND
(1844-1916)

ELIZA STICKLAND (NÉE CRUTCHER)
(1845-1918)

He inherited the Travellers Rest Inn at Three Legged Cross from his uncle Thomas Lukes. A man of many talents and notable public figure, he is listed as Innkeeper, Grocer, Accountant, Insurance Agent and Public Auditor. He was also Secretary then President of the Southern Counties Independent Order of Oddfellows.

Married W.P. Stickland in 1867. She was the daughter of Stephen and Charlotte. The Crutchers were a well established, successful Three Legged Cross family of pottery dealers, farmers and tradesmen who owned land between Verwood and Church Roads. William Peter and Eliza had ten children of whom a girl, Emeline, died young.

"Oakdene", Horton Road, Three Legged Cross built for William Peter and Eliza Stickland
at the end of the nineteenth century after they retired from the Travellers Rest Public House.
The site now contains a Nursing Home of the same name.

THE WEDDING PARTY OF FRED STEELE AND BESSIE ORMAN IN 1912
Bessie's parents, Priscilla and Charles are seated right of her in this photograph
which was taken at their home, Holly Tree Farm, Ringwood Road, Three Legged Cross

(HENRY) JAMES AND MARY JANE JOY (NÉE GRITT) AND FAMILY ABOUT 1914
James, a Market Gardener and Dealer, was both a first and second cousin to
Bessie, above, through their shared Orman ancestry.
Mary Jane was the daughter of William Gritt, Chimney Sweep and his wife Mary Sherred

THATCH COTTAGE

Bessie Steele, née Orman outside her home in Ringwood Road, Three Legged Cross. Bessie usually wore a man's cap and one of her occupations was to light the fires at the Congregational Chapel.

Fred was a Broommaker and had his thatched workshop behind the house. Both house and workshop remain today as picturesque dwellings.

PINE VIEW

On the corner of Lower Common and Ringwood Roads, this was the home of Eli Sherred and his wife Lucy Mary Dibben who married in 1905. Eli was a cousin of Mary Jane Joy née Gritt.

Their married daughter, Mrs. Hayter and her husband continued to live at the cottage.

WOOLSBRIDGE FARM

Now the Old Barn Farm Inn, this was the farmhouse where John Henry Joy (1845-1922) and his first cousin and wife Mary Jane Orman brought up their nine children. John was an uncle of James Joy.

Branches of the Joy family lived in several other parts of Three Legged Cross, amongst them Gundry's Farm and the site of the Joy's Farm housing estate.

PEOPLE AND PLACES

Matters were not all uneventful in Verwood and Three Legged Cross as the incident below demonstrates. Politics of the area were strongly Liberal and exception was taken on this occasion to a Conservative meeting as reported in a local newspaper on 25th February 1887. The incident became known as the "Mannington Scuffle".

GROSS POLITICAL OUTRAGE

A determined and preconcerted plan to break up a Primrose League meeting which was announced to take place in the National schoolroom, Mannington, near Verwood, Dorset, was made on Thursday evening, the 17th last. Mr. G. H. Bond, M.P. was announced to speak, and among others present were Mr. Brouncker, who presided, Mr. Parker, the organising secretary of the Conservative Association, and a party of vocalists who came by a conveyance from Wimborne.

There were early indications of opposition as the conveyance was met by a volley of stones. At the commencement of the proceedings the following letter from Mr. Bond was read:- "Dear Sir, I find it will be impossible for me to be at Mannington tomorrow. We are still debating the reply to the Queen's Speech, as we have been for the last 3 weeks, and today Mr. Smith has intimated that the Government will take steps to bring it to a close. Under these circumstances, the Whips refuse me leave of absence. I regret this very much as I should have liked to visit my friends in the Mannington district, who I am sure will excuse my absence, as the fate of the country depends upon the Government having the fullest support at the present juncture."

After this letter was read, a pianoforte recital was being given, when a shower of brickbats came through the windows and, throughout the recital, missiles were thrown at the doors and windows. Mr. Parker intimated that, as Mr. Bond was unable to be present, no political speeches would be made and he invited those outside to come in and spend a pleasant evening, but this invitation served only to further exasperate the offenders.

Matters ultimately became so serious that the meeting had to be stopped. On leaving the School-house the party were greeted with showers of stones and were forced to seek shelter in the house of Mrs. B....... where they remained for an hour and a half. The Wimborne conveyances, which were in the yard, were smashed. Two ladies were hurt and Mr. Tong, of Wimborne, who had come out to sing, and Mr. H. J. Eaton of Wimborne, the accompanist, were both injured in the face by missiles, Mr. Stanley Hayter also meeting with a blow in the leg. The assailants waited outside and found vent for their spite in breaking the windows of and in other ways damaging a carriage from Laing's Hotel, Wimborne, which had conveyed the party from that place.

Subsequently they drew off and from Statements made appear to have waited at a corner until the party should leave and drive away. The carriage, however, left in a direction other than expected but was followed some little distance by the yelling assailants, who again threw stones and brickbats, and there is very little doubt that one of their number fired a gun or firearm at the retreating carriage, as the driver and others speak to seeing the flash and the driver says he heard the shot or whatever it may have been whiz past the carriage. This ------ ------ made such an impression that one gentleman found it necessary to stay at the house all the night and he left the next morning.

There is a heap of stones in the room in which the entertainment was to have been given and a large quantity of window glass was broken. Some of the men were recognised and no doubt the ------- will in due time come before the Magistrates.

One assumes that the more respectable members of the community were not involved. Stephen Orman of Cob Cottage, Three Legged Cross, Trustee of the Congregational Church and a man of irreproachable integrity was a noted local Liberal. It is reported that when polling took place in the old Church School, the pupils conveyed the ballot papers to his house in Church Road to be counted. This practice would hardly be passed by the electoral scrutineers of today but casts a favourable light on the reliability of the chosen children.

PEOPLE AND PLACES

Pictured here are just a few of the many well remembered Verwood people of the twentieth century.

Left: Mr. Jesse Strawbridge, Headmaster of Verwood Council School.

Right: Mr. Robert John Stride, Assistant Master of the Council School. Mr. Stride had been in the Army Educational Corps in India. After his wife died in 1950 he married Lena Alice Watts, the Headmistress of the Church School.

Miss Lorna Limpus (1893-1971) a leading member, amongst others organizations, of the Girl Guide Association and the Parochial Church Council. She was always a stalwart champion of Verwood's rights.

Left: George Bailey, village barber for over fifty years, always had a smile and a friendly chat for his customers. He was Vice-Chairman and enthusiastic member of Verwood Historical Society with a fund of amusing and interesting stories of local incidents over the years.

Right: Miss Hilda Keene, the Church School Headmistress who preceded Miss Watts. Seen here with some of her younger pupils, Peggy Northeast, left, Eileen Holloway, right and Christine Henning, centre.

We shall be meeting these Verwood folk again together with many other local characters in a variety of situations on the following pages

THE CHURCHES

As a series of outlying agricultural hamlets, Verwood was never under the immediate eagle eye of a resident landowner or clergy. This allowed a strong non-conformist element to thrive alongside those adherents of the Church of England which division strengthened over the nineteenth century. Aided by separate schooling it led to two virtually co-existent communities of acquaintances and friends in which succeeding generations were raised.

On the Tithe Map of 1847 five religious establishments are shown. A church on the site of the present St. Michael & All Angels, a chapel in the keeping of the Society of Independents nearby on Church Hill or Hurdles Hill as it was then known, a chapel on Dewlands Common on land registered to Rebecca Shearing, a chapel in what is now Manor Road in the name of Thomas Bailey and a chapel in Ringwood Road, Three Legged Cross on land owned by Samuel Goulding.

The non-conformist "Independents" were the first to establish a place of worship in Verwood, followed a few years later by the Anglicans and then by the Methodists. Over the years there have been other religious foundations such as the Baptist Chapel which stood until the early twentieth century roughly opposite the present Monmouth Ash public house. When it was demolished clouds of bats flew out of its thatched roof. Services have also been held by the TocH in a small hut which stood on the site of the present Band Hall. It had a small Chapel at one end containing an altar, lamp, cross, banner and stained glass window.

Banner of the Verwood Rechabite Silver Star Tent

There was also a Rechabite "Silver Star" tent whose Secretary in 1946 was Mr. Job Sims of Honeysuckle Cottage, Newtown and whose members amongst other things were committed to teetotalism. Amongst mobile outreaches, Titcombe's Mission Tent stood on the corner of Moorlands and Edmondsham Roads. Evangelical congregations were established in the mid twentieth century in both Verwood and Three Legged Cross. In later years, the Salvation Army held its first meeting in Verwood in 1991 and a family church has since been founded. There has never been a Catholic Church in Verwood and those of this denomination worship at West Moors or Ringwood.

THE CHURCHES

THE ESTABLISHED CHURCH

For centuries the parishioners of Verwood and parts of Three Legged Cross had to travel between four and seven miles to the mother church of Cranborne to attend worship and for services of baptism, marriage and burial. In 1829 a petition of the 400 villagers called for a Chapel of Ease which was granted with a half acre Chapelyard on the site of what is now St. Michael and All Angels Parish Church. From then on, baptisms and burials could be conducted locally though it was never licensed for marriages. The land was purchased from William Rolles Fryer for the sum of five shillings and an annual rent of one peppercorn. It was reputedly a plain, mudwalled building, most probably thatched, with galleries along the north and west sides. It remained as such until a small brick chancel was added in 1870.

In 1886 in preparation for its new status of Parish Church the chapel was totally rebuilt in local brick and decorated with string courses of white Ebblake brick. The bricks were brought to the site in carts supplied by the Standfield family of Margards Lane.

The Restynge House in Ringwood Road opened August 1907

1887 saw the arrival of the first Vicar, Reverend Claud Brown, a dedicated man of private means, who was to have a great impact on Verwood. He was born in New South Wales in 1850 to a merchant family of Scottish origins who then returned to England where Claud later graduated from Wadham College, Oxford. He married a cousin, Marion Janet Wyld, in London in late 1875 and a son, Claud Leonard, was born in 1879, his wife sadly dying a fortnight after the birth. He married again at Salisbury, Wiltshire in 1882 to Georgina Florence Stephens Hyde, daughter of a Naval Commander, later having three children, Hubert, Audley and Joyce. Claud Brown had been curate of a parish in Kensington but he left these social climes to devote the rest of his working life to the souls of Verwood.

During his first few years in the village he built an imposing Vicarage, since demolished but thus giving Vicarage Road its name. The coach house and stables still stand as dwellings in Copse Road. He also had built "The Restynge House" opposite Ferrett Green as a social club and alternative to the pubs for the young men of the village. This was rebuilt in 1990 in similar but larger style and houses businesses including Bailey's Electrical shop.

THE CHURCHES

At St. Michael and All Angels, a fine new Bath stone Chancel was erected in 1892 and the church adorned with items of superior, delicate workmanship, some it is said carved by his wife's very talented niece, Florence Darke.

Claud Brown also had All Saints built at Three Legged Cross. It was an Iron Mission Church, known as the "Tin Church", opened on February 13th 1893. In 1957 the metal was clad in stone and faced inside with wood, which improved its appearance but eventually led to structural concern. In 1994 it was decided not to replace it traditionally but to create a complex of priest's house, church and meeting room dedicated on 14 January 1995.

All Saints and St. Mary's at West Moors, also built by Claud Brown, were served as necessary by curates and Vicar. However there was a strong non-conformist core in Verwood and little Christian love between the two factions. Children taunted each other as "churchy bugs" and "chapel bugs or brats", lying in wait for one another with clods of earth as they left their respective services.

As one Anglican who remembered Claud Brown put it, being of strong principles and convinced he was in the right "he didn't help" to narrow the gap. Happily these differences have long been resolved and the churches now work together in unity and harmony.

Verwood Parish Church dedicated to St. Michael & All Angels built 1886
Before it was rebuilt in 1980

45

THE CHURCHES

On a personal note, Claud Brown became great-uncle to the future 1950s television presenter Mary Malcolm through his sister Isabella who had married into the Malcolm family, Lairds of Poltalloch in Scotland. Isabella and her husband Edward had a son, later Sir Ian Malcolm who in 1902, at St. Margaret's, Westminster, had married Jeanne Marie, daughter of the "Jersey Lily" Lillie Langtry of Edwardian socialite fame. One wonders if Verwood knew of the tenuous relationship between their upright vicar and this somewhat notorious lady and if Claud and his wife Georgina had attended his nephew's wedding.

Rev. Claud Brown retired in 1917 after 30 years unstinting service to the church and parish having seen through the first three years of the Great War. By this time his health was broken and he was all but blind, reciting the services by heart. He would never use a carriage on Sundays but would walk to Three Legged Cross to take Evensong there. One night was so dark that he stumbled into the River Crane but still carried on to take his duty.

He preached his farewell sermon at a Sunday evensong on a text from the Psalms "Not unto us O Lord but unto Thy name be the praise". If memorial were needed it is surely in that Verwood has never forgotten him, his name still commanding love and respect whilst his gifts continue to adorn the parish church.

A succession of Vicars followed but the next major change came in 1980 in response to the growing population of Verwood. By the inspiration and dedication of Reverend Anthony Roberts and the congregation of the time, the whole of the body of the church was extended outwards leaving the original area as the central nave. A Meeting Room was added at the west end as an entrance hall and gathering place replacing an earlier small brick porch. The beautifully decorated chancel was left unchanged and in 2001 was repainted and gilded to stunning effect.

The churchyard has always been the burial place for all members of the community and indeed the first burial in January 1830 was that of John Adams, the first Minister and Preacher of the Independent Chapel which stood close by on Church Hill. His gravestone with a suitably admonitory warning stands just within the church gates. The bones of many parishioners of all stations in life lie side by side in this peaceful setting. A stone cross in the central path is a memorial to Rev. Claud Brown's first wife.

The churchyard was extended several times over the years until all available land was full and it became necessary for the Council to provide a Public Cemetery. Until the 1980 reorganisation, the churchyard had become completely overgrown and infested with brambles, gorse and weeds. Since the lack of plentiful manual labour in modern times it had been by no means an easy task to keep it tidy. In 1980 the old part of the churchyard was mapped and the names and dates on every visible grave recorded before a faculty was granted to remove some of the kerbs for ease of mowing. The gravestones were kept in their original positions as found at the time though a few had already been displaced and resited when the Memorial Garden for cremations was created at the entrance to the church in the 1960s.

St. Michael and All Angels Parish Church from the north side of the churchyard in the early 20th century
The brick nave was built in 1886 and decorated with white string courses of Ebblake Brick
The Bath Stone Chancel was added in 1892

The original interior of St. Michael and All Angels showing the beautifully stencilled walls
These were painted white in 1957 to give more light
The gas lamps were lit by the sidesmen but the choirboys used to
enjoy extinguishing them by blowing through a long tube

THE CHURCHES

THE CHURCH. THREE LEGGED CROSS.

ALL SAINTS

The daughter church of St. Michael and All Angels was built in 1893 to serve the inhabitants at the southern end of the parish.

In 1957 an architect who had recently come to live in Three Legged Cross suggested that All Saints should be clad in stone.

This brought an enthusiastic response with donations being speedily forthcoming. Whilst it undoubtedly improved its visual appearance, after nearly forty years it gave rise to structural concerns. The building was demolished in 1994 and a new complex of church, hall and living accommodation was built in its place.

THREE LEGGED CROSS METHODIST CHURCH

The Primitive Methodist Chapel in Ringwood Road, Three Legged Cross which was built in 1893 and taken out of service in 1984. The surrounding field was the scene of Open Air meetings.

THE CHURCHES

THE INDEPENDENT AND CONGREGATIONAL CHAPELS

Self respect had been restored to this impoverished area from 1802 onwards when a small Independent Chapel had been erected in Verwood and the ministers, themselves simple working men of the people, were held in great respect and love. The first Pastors were John Adams, followed by Jeremiah Argyle a whitesmith and David Brewer from Damerham. "Congregational Churches of Dorset" tells us that

> *"It was a wild and neglected district, quite destitute of the means of grace; whole families lived and died without being able to read the Scriptures or hear the gospel preached.... "A friend, whose name does not transpire, seeing the spiritual darkness and indifference that prevailed, was moved to erect a small place of worship, which was opened December 27th 1802."*

There are said to have been at least four Independent – later Congregational – churches in Verwood. The one on Dewlands Common may be the earliest chapel outgrown and replaced by that on Church Hill which was most likely of wooden construction. In 1877 the chapel which is now the Library was built in Manor Road on land provided by Squire Fryer and the latest is the present United Reformed Church next door. The opening service, attended by a large congregation, was held on Easter Monday 16th April 1906. This latter was erected in response to the difficulty of holding church services and a school in the same building especially when midweek funeral services were needed. On these occasions the children had to be sent home or crammed into a smaller room with strict admonitions to keep very quiet.

Opening Day of the new Chapel in Manor Road on Easter Monday 1906

One of the founding fathers was Job Brewer (seated far left), who was made a Life Deacon in 1924 in recognition of his 26 years as Treasurer in addition to his other services. Members of the Sims potting and building families were amongst other early members of the congregation. A full time Pastor was appointed from 1908.

One of the most fondly remembered institutions of the early twentieth century were the PSAs – Pleasant Sunday Afternoons of fellowship and church activity which enabled whole families to socialize on the strictly kept Sabbath. On fine days these were held in the Manor House gardens.

THE CHURCHES

In 1945 Rev. A. W. Williams became the first resident Minister, establishing himself also as a prominent and popular member of the village society.   There was an active Boys Brigade, Lifeboys, Youth Club and Junior Church and in 1963 the premises were extended for these and other activities.   In latter years there have again been alterations and improvements to the combined church and hall.   The congregation voted, along with the majority of Congregational Churches, to unite with the Presbyterian Church of England to become the United Reformed Church in 1972.

Three Legged Cross Congregational Church

In Three Legged Cross the origins of the Independent, later Congregational Chapel in this area appear to be on a quarter acre or "rood" plot owned in the early 19th century by Samuel Golding or Goulding on the south side of Ringwood Road at the side of his cottage. This property is still known as Chapel Farm, although rebuilt after a fire, and has been in existence from at least 1847 and probably for some years before.

According to the book "Congregational Churches of Dorset" in 1861 a better chapel was needed and was obtained on a leasehold site at a small rental from Lord Shaftesbury. Miss Carter of Ringwood who was also a substantial contributor to the later Verwood Chapel was the main benefactor, bearing the whole cost of £170 assisted by the congregation who contributed their own time and labour.   Despite the initial difficulties in Three Legged Cross, when the inhabitants reportedly preferred to spend their Sundays in drinking and fighting, the Chapel prospered.   Eventually a larger one was needed and a roadside site obtained from William Rolles Fryer on easy terms on the lives of William Hatchard, Stephen Orman and Jesse Stickland.   Gilbert D. Jennings Esq. of London laid the foundation stone in August 1890.   However, on 15th August 1890 Henry Golding gave a written receipt for £3 to Sam Thorne of the Congregational Building Committee for a quarter acre of his land for the site of the "above chapel" so it is not clear to whom the land belonged at this stage. Whatever the sequence of events, it is fairly certain that William Rolles Fryer opened the chapel on 19th May 1891 when he said a few words before Rev. John Ossian Davies of Bournemouth preached.   The building cost £360 and was paid for by 1894.   The Sunday School roll stood at 54 superintended by Mr. Barrett and that of the Band of Hope at 40.   The stables were built and paid for by those who drove there by horse and trap. A Day School of about 50 pupils supported by Miss Carter and afterwards by her nephew Reginald Jennings was held in the old chapel.

THE CHURCHES

THE METHODISTS

Methodist worship has been strong in Verwood for well over a hundred and fifty years. In 1847 it was mentioned as being in the Salisbury Circuit of the Primitive Methodist Church, though it is likely that worship was conducted in homes or barns. In 1853 Open Air Services were being held and a Primitive Methodist Chapel was erected in 1876 on the site of the present Methodist church which replaced it in 1909.

The old Primitive Methodist Chapel in Vicarage Road.

The land beyond was originally a small-holding belonging to Dan Sims, son of the smuggler, who left money for the parish bread charity. He used to organize apple races for the children in the roadway outside.

The houses opposite are built with string courses of white Ebblake Brick

The Methodists had their own music group in earlier times and there has been a thriving youth group enjoying many activities and outings. It was noted that on the 1940 annual outing to Christchurch the coach fare was £3 and the cost of tea £1.0.6d including one for the driver. There was also a Sunday School outing to Weymouth. The ladies of the congregation made hundreds of ham and boiled beef sandwiches but there were no cakes or biscuits. The Sunday School met twice on Sundays when verses of scripture were learned and repeated unaccompanied by any other activities.

At Three Legged Cross, a tiny brick Primitive Methodist Church was built in 1893 in a field in Ringwood Road on the site of a previous mud wall structure dating from about 1850. After some years rain had got into the cob walls and slowly conditions grew worse until one side collapsed. The trustees replaced it with a brick wall but their efforts to save the rest of the building were in vain and so a new one was built in its place.

Up to the First World War, Camp Meetings were held regularly in the open air paddock alongside the church and as many as 150 to 200 men and women would meet. They then marched to the public house where they halted and gave their invitation before marching back to the chapel, halting twice on the way. A wagon was drawn up in the chapel ground, the pulpit and harmonium lifted onto it and from there a team of local preachers conducted the service which lasted from morning until evening.

Transport from Poole, in whose Circuit it was then based, was extremely difficult but the problem was solved by having a special trap built which seated six preachers for six chapels in the circuit. During the Second World War matters were so difficult that the stewards often had to find their own preachers locally. In 1944 Three Legged Cross was transferred from the Poole Circuit to Wimborne.

In later years, falling congregations led to the Chapel being taken out of use in 1984 after which it stood empty for several years before being sympathetically extended and converted into an attractive private dwelling.

The imposing Methodist Church, incorporating a hall to the right, built 1909 in Vicarage Road.
It replaced the old Primitive Methodist Chapel on the same site. Later the surrounding brick wall
was removed and an exterior hall added in the rear grounds.

A larger, modern permanent Hall was added at the rear and opened on 4th February 1984. In 1993, under the ministry of Rev. Chris Blake, the church was extensively enlarged and redesigned with attractive glass panelled doors fronting the pavement. The "new" church reopened in January 1994.

The Methodist Music Group which played not only in Verwood but at surrounding churches

THE CHURCHES

THE EVANGELICAL CHURCHES

Several outreach Missions had visited Verwood from time to time but the first known permanent congregation was at the Foursquare Gospel Tabernacle sited on land at Hayward's Farm off Margards Lane. This was the forerunner of the Bethel Chapel and after the congregation had moved to a brick building the hall was sold to the members of the Three Legged Cross Evangelical movement in 1934.

The first known Evangelical Church in Verwood sited on land at Hayward's Farm

Bethel Chapel in Ringwood Road, Verwood was opened on 23rd April 1931 on land acquired for £50. It had previously been the site of Tent Missions. Two Verwood men, Godrick Sims and Clifford Sims who had attended Evangelical Meetings in Bournemouth came home and prayed over Lloyd Shearing, a chronically sick young man, who made a complete recovery. Lloyd's father Frederick became a committed Christian and he, Godrick and Clifford gave up their jobs in order to build Bethel accepting only £37 between them for labour. An official loan of £100 repayable over ten years was made followed by another of £82 the following year. When the Chapel opened it had to have three Sunday services to accommodate all those who wished to attend. The first Pastor was Winston Shearing and when he left his brother Lloyd succeeded him for twenty-five years.

Electricity was installed in 1935 when the application was signed by Winston Shearing, Gardener of Manor Lane, and witnessed by Frederick Prior. On 28th May 1954 the Chapel was registered to solemnize marriages. Further alterations and extensions were made and in 1991 the vestry and kitchen were added. In 2004 the old doorway was replaced by a porch.

The Bethel Chapel in Ringwood Road
Remains a Free Evangelical Church

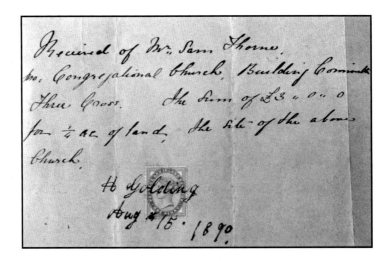

Left: Miss Sarah Orman (1871-1934) in "Sunday best" attending Three Legged Cross Congregational Church.
Above: Receipt from Henry Golding for a quarter of an acre of land for building the new church in 1890.

Left: Erecting the brand new chicken shed, purchased in 1939 which served for many years as Three Legged Cross Evangelical Church.

Below: A group of happy youngsters at a "Band of Hope" outdoor temperance meeting in June 1913.

THE CHURCHES

Members of the Orman and Harding families of Three Legged Cross were the principal founders of the Evangelical Church in Verwood Road, Three Legged Cross, known in its early days as The Gospel Hall. They had both been associated with the Brethren Assembly but lacking a local venue had worshipped at the nearby Congregational Chapel. In 1932 it was decided to form a separate congregation according to their own tenets and beliefs.

Baptism by full immersion in the Moors River at Woolsbridge

Two years later the second-hand creosoted hut known as the Foursquare Gospel Tabernacle was purchased for the sum of £10 from the Verwood congregation and erected on the land of George and Elsie Harding at Vine Cottage. Visiting preachers would cycle many miles in all weathers in order to minister to the small congregation. From the start a missionary outlook on life, both home and abroad, was strongly encouraged. This no doubt was the seed of Joyce Harding's lifetime of service in India and the very popular, well attended summer Bible School which Frank and Georgina (neé Harding) Rowdon later held in their large garden at St. Margaret's, Station Road, Verwood now "The Oaks".

By 1939 a grant of £150 had enabled the purchase of a brand new deep litter wooden poultry shed which, never used for its original purpose, provided enlarged and upgraded premises. Marriages were conducted within but there was no baptistery. Baptisms were carried out at neighbouring assemblies or more often by full immersion in the River Crane at Woolsbridge. The older building was moved to serve as a hall and remained as such until 1976.

By 1972 it was decided that a new purpose built meeting place was needed and so a well supported Building Fund commenced. This culminated in the opening of the present permanent brick building in late 1976, a testament to the faith and perseverance of that early, small congregation.

The above is only a short précis of its history as the full, fascinating story of the church and its people is told by Ken Orman in his book "In a Small Village" published 2004.

Incidentally, family research relates that the origin of the Orman surname in Dorset appears to be through Miles Ormandy, Parish Clerk of Hampreston, in the 17th century, who was associated with the Vicar Miles Bowness, appointed in 1614. They both came from the area of present day Cumbria and may have been kinsfolk. The name was contracted to Orman in the early 18th century.

THE SCHOOLS

The first school in Verwood was built in 1847 by the Anglican "National Society" on land at Church Hill donated for the purpose by Squire William Rolles Fryer. It was a brick building designed to accommodate 120 children with a teacher's house attached. It served as one of the village primary schools until 1985 when the staff and pupils moved to new premises in Howe Lane. The building has now been converted into St. Michael and All Angels Parish Centre. Prior to this the children had been taught in the nearby church for ten years and there had also been informal "Dame's Schools" for rudimentary education. Schooling was not free until 1891 but cost a few pence a week towards the teacher's salary, part of which was deemed to include the occupancy of the schoolhouse. This was most probably a strain on the budget of several parents as well as being a source of financial anxiety to the Head Teacher.

The two Chapels in Manor Road, the one on the right built in 1877 and the one on the left in 1906
In front stands the commemorative oak planted for the Coronation of George VI
which was felled in 2006 during road alterations and a replacement planted on Ferrett Green

Shortly after the Church School was established, the non-conformist villagers started their own classes which in 1880 became the "British School" held in the 1877 chapel in Manor Road. After the adjacent chapel was built in 1906 it occupied the whole premises and continued as a County Senior School and later additional primary school until a replacement was opened in Hillside Road in 1967. It is now the Verwood Library.

At Three Legged Cross a National School and schoolhouse, which could be used as a church when occasion demanded, was built in 1873 in Church Road, then called Silver Street. It was followed a year later by an interdenominational school in School Lane off Ringwood Road. Until that time the children of this area had to walk to school in Verwood crossing the River Crane near Manor Farm by a plank bridge. This route was impassable in severe weather and mothers frequently kept their younger children at home in winter months.

The Church School at Three Legged Cross closed in 1964, merging with the Chapel or Council School. A brand new replacement building has since been built in Church Road, not far from the site of the original Anglican School and was opened on 12th October 1979 as Three Legged Cross First School.

THE SCHOOLS

Higher education was provided for boys at Queen Elizabeth's School, Wimborne and for girls at Parkstone Grammar School for those children who passed the Scholarship Examination. The advent of the Comprehensive system saw Verwood children over the age of nine educated at either Cranborne or West Moors Middle Schools progressing to Wimborne or Ferndown Upper Schools. There was no provision for further education in the village until Emmanuel Middle School was built in Howe Lane, under the auspices of Salisbury Diocese, in 1990. More recently Trinity First School opened its doors in 2001 to provide much needed additional accommodation for the growing junior population at the northern end of the parish. This school started its life in a mobile classroom in the rear garden of Verwood Methodist Church who had offered it this temporary home until the permanent buildings were completed off Coopers Lane where it is now firmly established.

VERWOOD NATIONAL SCHOOL

The school opened its doors on 7th October 1847 under the Headship of Mrs. Elizabeth Sims, wife of Stephen, a Railway Gateman from Manswood near Moor Crichel. At that time the nearest railway ran through Ringwood and West Moors to Wimborne but by April 1861 he had given up that employment and was a Sawyer at Three Legged Cross, with his wife having no profession apart from her home and family.

Elizabeth, neé White, born at Edmondsham, must have come from an educated family as a sister was also a schoolmistress. She came to the school aged 26 with two small daughters. During her thirteen or so years as Head Teacher she gave birth to four more children whilst managing to present her brighter pupils for the Salisbury Diocesan Examinations with some success.

Over the years there was a succession of teachers many of whom stayed only a short time as they climbed the career ladder or became despondent at the numerous difficulties presented in trying to educate rural children according to various government dictates.

School log books, to be entered each day by the Head Teacher, were introduced in 1862 and Verwood Church School was fortunate in retaining a complete set, now deposited for safe keeping in Dorset History Centre at Dorchester.

As well as recording school events these form a fascinating village diary detailing weather, employment exigencies, festive occasions, epidemics and other events of major and minor note which give a rounded picture of local life.

To overcome the initial problem of finding sufficient educated adults willing to become teachers, a Monitorial and a Pupil Teacher system was used with the Head giving instruction out of school hours to the older, brighter pupils who in turn passed their knowledge on to their juniors.

Although the state was not directly involved in education until 1870, grants were made to assist in the running of the schools and so of course Inspections were made to ensure the money was being well spent.

THE SCHOOLS

The first recorded Examination of Verwood National School in 1854 was by the Reverend E. D. Tinling who commented that

"the attendance of the children in this wild district is very good
and reflects great credit on the teacher and apprentice".

Verwood Church School at the rear of the Parish Church
Taken in the 1920s after the Schoolhouse had been extended to over double its original size

At this time grants were on a capitation basis of three to six shillings per pupil subject to a minimum of 176 days attendance. On the day of inspection there were 141 children present, greatly surpassing the general average over later years. Indeed, accommodation had only been provided for 21 less than that number so it must have been a tremendous squeeze to fit them all in. One cannot help but wonder if some sort of inducement had been offered to the children in order to guarantee their attendance when the Inspector called.

Later, a system of "Payment by Results" was a grievous burden to the teachers when the school budget depended on the standard reached by the children in an annual examination supplemented by their fees out of which had to come not only the teacher's salary but the running expenses. Unsurprisingly, even after months of careful teaching and drilling in basic subjects, the children frequently "went to pieces" when confronted by an alien examiner. In 1890 Mr. Edwin Mann despairingly wrote "It seems hopeless to get a good report in this school after all the grinding they have had during the past year, but I see looking back through the old log book, the complaint is these children never do themselves justice on examination day, and yet I do not see the grant ever exceeded when the average was much higher and before the Chapel school was built". Education was not entirely compulsory until 1880 whilst free education did not come into force until 1st September 1891.

Mr. Charles Daintree, who only remained as Head of the school for a year and eight months, resigned on this very point in 1881 after receiving a letter from the Vicar of Cranborne, also Correspondent Manager of the school, which told him that "It is evident that the subscriptions and school pence cannot, even with a larger grant than we have lately received, meet the expenditure of the school and it will be necessary to reduce the salary of teachers considerably". He left behind in the Schoolhouse one bedstead, two dressing tables, two tables downstairs, two washstands and one chest of drawers which presumably were the property of the parish and the only furnishings provided. The 1891 census finds the family at Horsham in Sussex where hopefully conditions were more satisfactory.

THE SCHOOLS

Heavy rain and snow brought only minimal attendance as many had inadequate clothing and there were no facilities for drying clothes when then reached school. The room was minimally warmed in the winter months and even at the coldest times there was sometimes difficulty in obtaining fuel so that it had to go unheated, often for weeks. The situation had not improved by 1907 when the teacher reported with !!! that the temperature at 9 a.m. was 31°F. On 27th January 1865 only four boys and two girls attended out of a roll of some one hundred pupils.

Some of the worst winters were in the 1880s. In the winter of 1880/81 the snow lay three or four feet deep in places and drifted to five or six feet suspending all the traffic. In January Mr. Daintree reported that the thaw set in, accompanied by rain. In consequence the school was flooded by melted snow coming through the roof. He wrote "My wife and I were up all night, bailing out the water from our bedroom which has greatly damaged the walls and furniture. It is impossible to hold school in the present flooded state of the schoolroom". At this time they were trying to get the children ready for the annual examination.

Boys frequently had to stay at home to help with gardening and seasonal farming jobs when their casual employment brought in much needed revenue. Harvest time was marked by a month's holiday for this purpose but even so the older boys, especially the farmers' sons, were weeks late back at school. Teas and treats were often laid on to tempt the children back to their lessons. Mr. David Jones reported in the early 1870s that "As a rule (without a single exception) in this school, children of the farmer class are more backward and more irregular in their attendance than any other". Even in the late 1890s a Captain Burbage had no compunction in employing the boys as beaters for his numerous shoots during school hours. The curriculum which these country children were expected to learn was often way above their heads. One mother called at the school begging that her son Oliver should not continue to "learn the poetry – it being too much for him".

Although only the worst misdemeanors were recorded, the behaviour of some of the children left a lot to be desired. They were very roughly spoken with swearing rife equally amongst the girls as the boys. Mrs. Mary Measures recorded on her first day as Headmistress in 1867 "I found the discipline to be most defective. I succeeded in gaining silence several times though with great difficulty. Throughout the school each child seems to follow the bent of its own inclination".

The earliest known photograph of the Church School
Taken about 1872 when Naomi Haskell, far left, was in her fourth and final year as Pupil Teacher

THE SCHOOLS

Before the week was out Sam Davis had struck Charles Ingram on the head with a slate and cut it badly. A few children were habitually impertinent and were sent or went home, returning with a parent or older sister to offer further abuse. She was further horrified when she caught Henry Sims and Herbert Haskell undressed and playing without their clothes on in the dinner hour. Offenders were reproved whenever possible but if this had no effect were caned on the spot or, more drastically, suspended until the Vicar, the final arbiter, was acquainted with the case.

In earlier days long illnesses, many of an epidemic nature, also hindered the learning process. Mr. Jones recorded in January 1870 that "Fanny Knowlton" who returned today after a long absence (she had the fever) has forgotten the whole of her arithmetic". "Fever", not specified, swept the village from 1869 to 1871 taking the lives of several children and near relatives. In November 1869 Mr. Jones tells that "A regular panic has taken place with regard to the fever. The school today was almost empty". After a prolonged absence by two of his brightest pupils he comments that "It is remarkable the facility with which children forget what they learn". It was not uncommon for children to have months off school with diphtheria, scarlet fever, bronchitis, measles, whooping cough, mumps, chickenpox or influenza. The school was closed on numerous occasions until the illnesses subsided.

On many pages it is recorded with sorrow that one of the pupils had died, sometimes very unexpectedly after having attended the previous week. The teacher always attended the child's funeral and in 1886 when a six year old girl, Katie Thorne, died "She was followed by the schoolchildren, many of whom put crosses and wreaths and white flowers on her coffin". From 1871 to 1896, Dr. Arthur Vann of Cranborne called regularly to vaccinate the children leading eventually to a regular programme of medical and dental preventative care.

Often absences were caused by more pleasurable pursuits. Though life for the children in the nineteenth century was harsh by our standards, in country districts it was by no means all depressing. There were no mines or factories to imprison them and in Verwood at that time a great deal more open space to roam in. Often the attractions of the fields, woods and streams exercised a greater call than that of learning. They swam in the river pools, sailed on the village ponds and in frozen winters, dallied skating on the ice.

The duckpond in Dewlands Road was no doubt a favourite spot for children to linger and play

THE SCHOOLS

They scrumped in the orchards, a convenient one near the school being raided by twelve year old Blanche Read in 1867. At Verwood and Ringwood Fair times there was scarcely an older child at the school and half holidays were usually given. Even a treat for the Chapel Sunday School meant that the Church School emptied rapidly. In 1895 many children absented themselves to visit the Army who were on manœuvres in the New Forest.

Any organized outing was prized to the full, even if only a tea and band concert on the Vicar's lawn. In September 1888 Reverend Brown organized a treat for his schoolchildren throughout the parish when children arrived from Three Legged Cross and West Moors and were led from Verwood School by the Drum and Fife Band to the marquee in the Vicar's field. Mr. Alfred Lenthall, Headmaster, describes a blissful occasion when a tea feast was held on Wednesday 29th September 1875, Patronal Festival of St. Michael and All Angels.

"Mr. Hayter supplied 144 lbs of spice cake and lent his field. On Tuesday afternoon and evening the children brought flowers and on Wednesday morning many of them came to assist the Sunday School teachers in decorating the room. At 1.30 the children arrived and began to form the procession to church where Mr. Boag (curate) held a little service at 2 p.m. and addressed the children. At 4.30 p.m. the children had tea in Mr. Hayter's field (Mr. Hayter was the landlord of the New Inn opposite the church) having carried the desks out for that purpose. The weather being all that we could wish. At 6.30 the races and scrambles ceased, the procession reformed for church where "Sun of my Soul" was sung and the Benediction given after which "Hark, Hark my Soul" was sung as a recessional and the children filed out, each child receiving a cake to carry home. The attendance was very poor on Thursday. Work scarcely satisfactory for a week."

In later years an annual excursion was made, usually to Bournemouth, at first by horse and brake, the journey there and back being part of the enjoyment and taking longer than the time thus allowed on the beach. It must have been a whole new country to some journeying through Three Legged Cross, West Moors, Ferndown, Kinson or Winton and finally the excited anticipation as they approached the sea.

Isaac and Bertha Benwell in their last year at the Church School in 1904
The lady standing far left may be Miss Way, the greatly loved Infants' Teacher
who was tragically killed in March 1919 when her bicycle collided with a coal lorry on Romford Hill
The school was given a half holiday so that the elder children might be taken in brakes to
Woodlands to form part of her funeral procession

THE SCHOOLS

In 1893 Mr. Isaac Benwell, assisted by his wife Bertha, arrived to take charge of the school. They remained for over eleven years and succeeded in raising the standards to a height not thought possible in earlier years. Education was now an established part of life and the status of teachers was improving.

At a time when most children had to leave school at the earliest opportunity to gain employment or help at home, it was encouraging that some Head Teachers, after a full day in the classroom, opened the door again at nights to give evening classes to such boys as might be inclined to further study. This enterprise had mixed results, the more studious being frequently interrupted by trouble makers and all exiting only to be mocked and pelted by those who no doubt considered them fair targets for trying to get above themselves. It needed a certain amount of courage and persistence in order to try and better oneself in those days.

Miss Isabella Mary Ellis, Headmistress from 1918 to 1923
She resigned "Having arrived at that age at which a pension becomes possible"
The late Mr. Aubrey Barrow, who gave so many reminiscences and photographs
to Verwood Historical Society, is standing in the back row at the far left

Later well remembered Head Teachers at the school included Mr. "Joey" Gatehouse "a man of uncertain temper" who fascinated the children by banging his fist on the desk until the bell crept nearer and nearer the edge. They hung with bated breath until it fell "with a great clatter". Later came Miss Isabella Mary Ellis then Miss Hilda Keene. Under the latter's headship, a major reorganization took place in 1932 when the Church School was designated the Junior School of the village with the Chapel School serving as the Senior, children transferring at the age of 9 and later 8.

Next in 1938 came Miss Lena Alice Watts who married the Assistant Master of the Senior School, becoming Mrs. R. J. Stride in 1952. As Headmistress during the War Years, she had to accommodate nearly sixty evacuees from Southampton plus their teacher, swelling the school roll to 148. Even after the War the school roll was too high so from 1951 to 1953 an Infant's Class was held at the Restynge House. Mrs. Stride remained Headmistress until 1961 at that time by far the longest serving. Then followed Miss Marie Grist and from 1968 until 1985, when the school transferred premises, the very enthusiastic Mrs. Patricia Hood ably assisted by Mrs. Georgina Miller and a succession of supplementary teachers. The new school premises opened in Howe Lane under the Headship of Mrs. Fiona Brown.

THE SCHOOLS

VERWOOD CHURCH SCHOOL

A reminder of the days in the 1940s and 50s when the class sat facing the teacher at rows of double desks with pen and pencil ridge, inkwell and lift up book locker.

Miss L. A. Watts was the Headmistress during this era.

On the left sits a youthful Michael D. Guy now a successful businessman and founder of M. D. Guy and Son, Electrical Contractors, on the Ebblake Industrial Estate.

VERWOOD C. OF E. FIRST SCHOOL – 8TH JUNE 1976 IN THE SCHOOL FIELD

BACK ROW: 1. Anita Sheldon 2. Teresa Dance 3. Amanda Whitfield 4. Emma Gash 5. Melanie Galton 6. Suzanne Allen 7. Tracey Tiller 8. Deborah Mills 9. Jackie Norton 10. Janis Froud 11. Kate Bowen 12. Katie Sullivan 13. Christine Bugden 14. Alison Foreman 15. Maria Stanton

4TH ROW: 1. Keith Miller 2. James Edgar 3. David Foster 4. Richard McDermott 5. Terry Sims 6. Malcolm Alcock 7. Martin Turner 8. Richard Collins 9. Christopher Frost 10. Andrew Brewer 11. Barry Percy 12. Andrew Mouland 13. Peter Swansborough? 14. Richard Martin 15. Simon Harris

3RD ROW: 1. Margaret Cutler 2. Emma Knight 3. Catherine Rowley 4. Sandra Mills 5. Keith Cox 6. Dawn Lock 7. Teresa Eames 8. Tina Kinder 9. Carmen Homfray 10. Shanta Smith 11. Diane Bugden 12. Christina Bicknell 13. Richard Norton 14. John Sims?

2ND ROW: 1. Robert Homfray 2. Greg Smith 3. Alistair Galton 4. Matthew Edgar 5. Paul Brewer 6. Warren Lock 7. Miss Irene Gill 8. Mrs. Patricia Hood, Headteacher 9. Mrs. Georgina Miller 10. Mary Gash 11. Anne-Marie Percy 12. Deborah Miller 13. Claire McDermott 14. Beverley Old 15. Sharon Turner

FRONT ROW: 1. Ruth Martin 2. Annabel Frost 3. Unidentified 4. Tina Albray 5. Stuart Harris 6. Sharon Bakewell 7. Wendy Tiller 8. Unidentified Foreman? 9. David Walbank 10. Unidentified 11. Daniel Sutton 12. Susannah Martin 13. Yvonne Atyeo

THE LAST TRADITIONAL MAY FESTIVAL HELD AT THE OLD CHURCH SCHOOL IN 1985
Michelle Harley was the May Queen

Maypole Dancing after the procession and ceremony

VERWOOD CHAPEL, LATER COUNCIL, SCHOOL

Although copies were made locally of the school log books before being taken for safe keeping at Dorset Record Office, the Chapel School records do not appear to have survived from as early as those of the Church School. However, we do learn that the Verwood Council School started evening classes in 1907 and on 1st November a Public Tea with a Lantern Lecture was held to gather intending pupils, both boys and girls, together. Views of London and Dorset were shown. The first session took place three days later when twenty pupils were present during which the Headmaster's wife, Mrs. Jessie Austen, took Needlework. Mr. Arthur Hopkins of the Verwood & Gotham Brick and Tile Works, who was one of the Managers of the School, attended.

Mr. George Watts Austen was Head Teacher of Verwood Undenominational "Chapel" school in the early twentieth century. On the 1901 census, when aged 35, he was described as "Schoolmaster, Journalist & Preacher of the United Methodist Free Church".

Excitement must have been rife in Verwood on 12th October 1908 when it was recorded that no evening school was held owing to the visit of H.R.H. and also a public meeting at the Chapel. Mr. Arthur Wareham, a former pupil of the Church School, recalled that "in 1908 the Prince and Princess of Wales visited the Wimborne St. Giles Estate for the shooting season – they later became King George V and Queen Mary. They arrived by train at the station and drove in a motor vehicle, of which few were seen around Verwood, to the St. Giles Manor. The day they left was a Public Holiday and the children of both schools lined the road around the station. As the carriage and horse procession of the Prince and Princess with all the local gentry approached the station, my school started singing a hymn which we had learned especially for the occasion. But the other school started cheering and because their school was bigger than ours, our singing was drowned." At the age of 80, this sad recollection still brought a tear to his eye.

Schoolchildren lined up outside the Albion Hotel to greet Royalty arriving at Verwood Station
The girls are wearing hats for the occasion and all are in their best clothes

THE SCHOOLS

The Day School Log Books are found from 1921 and record for the main part the usual day to day running of a school. Inspection Reports were not very complimentary at this stage and there seems to have been a succession of supply teachers. However, on 6th January 1931 Mr. Alec Harold Marsh arrived to take charge. A House System was introduced with the children divided amongst Canada, India, Africa and Australia. The championship was to be decided on work, conduct, attendance and sport with the children taking a keen interest.

In May 1936, as Verwood Senior Mixed School, it was reported that "Work is still carried on in premises which have long been regarded as defective and unsuitable. It is a matter for relief that the erection of a new building has been definitely decided on by the Local Education Authority and it is hoped that this will be pressed forward with all possible speed". Unfortunately the Second World War intervened and it was not until 1967 that the much longed for replacement was built in Hillside Road.

In March 1937 it was impossible to use the large room owing to the heating stove smoking. The girls of Class I had to share the small room with Class III whilst those of Class II were occupied elsewhere at a Domestic Science lesson. Classes I and II boys were taken to Games in the Recreation Ground. This occasion may have been a natural occurrence but later on "boys" have admitted that they knew how to make the stove smoke when they wished to avoid lessons for the greater pleasures of outdoors!

At the Council School also in the 1930s relations between school and adjacent chapel were strained. The children kicked footballs and other balls onto the roof and damaged slates. The church wanted a Council contribution for the repairs.

In December 1937 Mr. Robert John Stride took up the post of Assistant Master whilst that of the Head was taken in October 1941 by Mr. Jesse James Strawbridge. The war years ensued during which Mr. Stride was commended on several occasions for his prompt assistance in emergencies. When the school transferred to Hillside Road 1967 the school Houses were Nelson and Wellington. The much loved Headmaster was Mr. Roy Cottrell supported by various teachers who became familiar to the new intake there. When the three tier educational system was introduced in 1973 it became Hillside County First School and is now known as Hillside Community First School. Hillside School was very fittingly opened by Roy Price, a former Chapel School pupil, by then the Dorset County Education Officer.

Hillside School. Rev. A. W. Williams presents a slide projector to retiring teacher Iris Thomson.
Headmaster Mr. Roy Cottrell centre

THE SCHOOLS

VERWOOD COUNCIL SCHOOL
Mr. George Watts Austen and some of his pupils outside the new Chapel about 1906

VERWOOD COUNCIL SCHOOL 1912

BACK ROW: 1. Jim Sims 2. Unidentified 3. Jimmy Shearing 4. Rupert Sims 5. Joe Read 6. Philip Warwick 7. ? Sims
8. Bernard Sims 9. Arthur Sims 10. Charlie Bailey

3RD ROW: 1. Bessie Bailey 2. Flora Bailey 3. Ada Spray 4. Dulcie Sims 5. Kathleen Sims 6. ? Thorne 7. Mary Thorne
8. Eva Bailey 9. Elsie Warwick 10. Unidentified 11. Mr. Austen, Headmaster

2ND ROW: 1. Nellie Bailey 2. Renie Sims 3. Unidentified 4. Hilda Shutler 5. Winnie Sims 6. Unidentified 7. Unidentified
8. Bertha Sims

FRONT ROW: 1. Cyril Alexander 2. Charlie Fry 3. Harold Ferrett 4. Ken Brewer 5. Bertie Reeks 6. Ben Spray 7. John Brewer

THE SCHOOLS

VERWOOD COUNCIL SCHOOL 1922

BACK ROW: 1. Arthur Poolman 2. Stanley Sims 3. Stanley Barrow 4. Frank Poolman 5. Les Barrow
6. Tom Kendall 7. Sid Cousins 8. Joe Davis?

MIDDLE ROW: 1. George Hopkins 2. Unidentified 3. Florrie Kendall 4. Madge Woods 5. Mabel Whitehorn 6. ? Robbins
7. Maud Haskell 8. Unidentified 9. Sybil Middleton 10. Hope Shearing 11. Josie Shearing

FRONT ROW: 1. Clarence Cosgrove 2. Cyril Webber 3. Harold Middleton 4. Fred Oxford 5. Unidentified
6. Renie Chiverton 7. George Budden 8. Stella Brewer 9. Reg Cox

VERWOOD COUNCIL SCHOOL 1931

BACK ROW: 1. Stanley Palmer 2. Jim Lockyer 3. Ron Shearing   4. Wilfred Sims 5. Gerald Froud 6. Bob Oliver
7. Roy Barrow   8. Monsell Shearing

3RD ROW: 1. Vera Groves 2. Dorothy Martin? 3. Marjorie Bailey 4. Bessie Sims 5. Jessie Ferrett 6. Lily Bumstead
7. Miss Riddle

2ND ROW: 1. Rosie Prior 2. Rosemary Thorne 3. Edna Shearing   4. Betty Tanner

FRONT ROW: 1. Jim Churchill 2. Reg Lockyer 3. Tom Barrow 4. Reg Smith 5. Alwyn Stainer 6. Roy Price

THREE LEGGED CROSS CHURCH SCHOOL

Three Legged Cross Church School in Silver Street, later Church Road

The Log Books preserved begin on 23rd November 1910 when there were 30 children present. The Vicar, Rev. Claud Brown, gave his weekly scripture lesson to the first class whilst the previous day the School Manager, Mr. William Peter Stickland had called to check the registers.

In February 1912 Cookery classes were to be held at West Moors and the girls from this school invited to attend for the whole day so that they would miss their normal lessons. Some parents thought it too far for the girls to walk but E. Orman and E. Dymond wished to go. It had an inauspicious start as they arrived for the first session only to find that the teacher had been taken ill and the class cancelled.

Verwood schoolgirls had their cookery lessons in a hut on Station Road which was also used for the boys' woodworking classes. One doubts that hygiene practices would allow such a mixture today however thoroughly the room was cleaned between sessions. By 1928 girls from the Three Legged Cross schools attended the classes there too. One former pupil recalled being taught how to skin and clean a rabbit only to lose hold and watch it float away down the nearby stream. One hopes her parents were not relying on it for their dinner.

In 1913 it was reported that the fourteen infant children were taught in the small sitting room of the Church School teacher's house and it was recommended that this practice should cease and that they should only be taught in the schoolroom. The next year the same room was still being used for sixteen children for which it was declared entirely unsuitable. The cramped conditions of the school were commented on many times over the years in that all age groups had to be taught within the same undivided room. Presumably the use of the teacher's sitting room was an unorthodox attempt to alleviate this problem though not appreciated by the authorities.

On 21st July 1915 the registers were not marked in the afternoon as only twelve children came back after lunch. "Mrs. H. Phillips was foolish enough to tell the children after morning school, that a flying machine had alighted on the common and they, childlike, rushed off to see it. When they got back it was too late for school."

It does not take much imagination to realize which the children preferred and no doubt they blessed the lady in question whatever the official view of the matter was. More officially a holiday was granted on 19th June 1922 when it was found that nearly half the children would be away on the occasion of a local wedding and a fête.

There appeared to be a great turnover of teaching staff and this was reported in the January 1923 Inspection Report with the added comment that the two Head Teachers who have been in charge had little experience of rural schools.

In January 1926 two sisters were removed by their parents and sent to the Undenominational School for the reason that they objected to C. of E. teaching and Country Dancing which appear linked together as twin evils!

The Portman Hunt met at "The Travellers Rest" in February 1933 for the first time in about twenty years and all scholars whose parents requested permission for their children to be present were allowed half an hour to go to see the meet. However, this must have become a more frequent occurrence as the children were again allowed out for the same purpose the following November.

Flying machines made another appearance on 29th November 1934 when the parents of over fifty per cent of the children requested they be excused school that afternoon "in order that they may witness passenger aeroplane flights, by Air Mails Ltd. at Potterne". This was more sympathetically treated than the former occasion and the school was closed at midday.

The War years followed, the School Log Book giving interesting insights into activities and effects which are amplified in a later chapter.

The 1944 Education Act showed its first effects when on 3rd March 1945 nine of the children were conveyed to Wimborne to sit for the Special Place Examination, colloquially known as "The 11 Plus". On 15th June it was recorded that Thomas W. Payne and Walter Rutt had been accepted for entrance to the Wimborne Grammar School.

On 2nd June 1954, the school was closed in the afternoon to enable the Headmistress, Miss M.A. Cope, to attend the official opening of Wimborne Secondary School which many children from all over the surrounding area would attend over the ensuing years. When the comprehensive system of education was introduced and the old Wimborne Grammar School closed these were amalgamated as Queen Elizabeth's School, known locally to all as "Q.E.".

Many incidents of misdemeanours of a playful or more serious nature are recorded but delicacy prevents revealing the culprits' names in later years. However, on 20th March 1956 "The man who brings the school dinners asked a small boy to open the school gates for him. The child refused to do so, so the man drove the van into the gate breaking a wooden stake". It seems that both child and adult parties here share the blame. In 1953 when a girl broke a window pane in the school for the second time, the exasperated teacher declared "she is like a lad!!!"

In July 1962 it was suggested that the school give up its independent diocesan status and become "controlled" by having the Council put in charge. There were so many repairs necessary and no money to pay for them. This situation was only resolved after several anxious discussions when it was decided to close the school completely and send the children to the council run County School off Ringwood Road. A temporary mobile classroom allowed the extra children to be accommodated there and the Church School closed its doors for the last time on 17th December 1964. Miss Cope had then been Head Teacher for the past eleven years.

The Chapel, later Council School, had of course run concurrently with the Church School for many years and, as in Verwood, was attended by those pupils whose parents did not approve of Anglican based education or otherwise found it convenient. It was situated in School Lane, off Ringwood Road and has since been converted to a private dwelling.

Whit Mondays in the non-conformist fraternity were particularly looked forward to as occasions of joyfulness and festivity. Church processions took place whilst a fête with swingboats and other attractions was held in the Chapel School grounds.

THE SCHOOLS

THREE LEGGED CROSS UNDENOMINATIONAL SCHOOL 1932

BACK ROW: 1. Joan Read 2. Mabel Golding 3. Olive Bailey 4. Lily Dymond 5. Marjory Shearing 6. Daisy Joy 7. Muriel Joy

3RD ROW: 1. Minnie Joy 2. Stella Golding 3. May Davis 4. Nora Joy 5. Doreen Steele 6. Rosie Sherred 7. Mary Drew 8. Gladys Sammars 9. Eileen Wood 10. Iris Dymond

2ND ROW: 1. Mary Sherred 2. Molly Keeping 3. Kathleen Sherred 4. Dorothy Steele 5. Dolly Bailey 6. Lily Orman 7. Olga Joy 8. Edna Sammars

FRONT ROW: 1. Betty Davis 2. Doris Joy 3. Rita Buckthorpe 4. Joan Davis 5. Doris Golding 6. Edna Bailey

TEACHERS: Left. Miss F. M. Foote   Right. Miss Saunders

HILLSIDE SCHOOL – 17TH DECEMBER 1997

After a rare Verwood snowfall the children certainly know how to enjoy themselves

30TH JULY 1986

Princess Margaret at the opening of the new Church First School

SICKNESS AND HEALTH

As in many country districts, health care was very rudimentary in the earlier days and mostly dependent on the local "wise women" who could prescribe herbal cures as well as attending at childbirth and deathbed. The nearest doctor was at Cranborne though he no doubt visited his outlying patients on horseback from time to time and could be summoned in emergencies. In any case, there was very little money available to pay fees. No doubt presents were often made in kind of the produce available as an alternative to money.

Until 1834 the Overseers of the Poor, arranged on a parochial basis, allowed basic relief to those too sick to work or support themselves. From then onwards there was no recourse apart from the Workhouse, the nearest situated in Wimborne some ten miles distant.

On the 1891 census a local woman, the widowed Maria Bailey, describes herself as a Sick Nurse though it is highly doubtful that she was trained. On the same census the 15 year old Bessie Orman of Woolsbridge is also recorded as a Nurse though that might have applied just to the 81 year old grandmother with whom she was living. In 1901 there were two pairs of sisters, Mabel and Fanny West, aged 17 and 14 who described themselves as Sick Nurse and Domestic Nurse respectively whilst Mary and Ellen Sims aged 31 and 26 were Monthly Nurses. A fifth Nurse boarding in Verwood though born at Horton was Emily West aged 36.

Rev. Claud Brown from 1887 onwards had organised a church based health and nursing service probably sufficient in those days to cover the much smaller population in a rudimentary fashion. In addition he provided a wheelchair in which those too sick to walk could be pushed by relatives to visit the doctor in Cranborne. This would hardly be regarded as acceptable today but was no doubt very gratefully received at the time.

THE CLOCK AND INFIRMARY, SALISBURY.

Right of the Clock Tower is the old Salisbury Infirmary near Fisherton Bridge. It closed at the end of 1992 with wards transferred to the new Salisbury District Hospital at Odstock. The site has now been re-developed as flats.

Those requiring hospital treatment were taken to Salisbury Infirmary or the Royal Victoria Hospital in Boscombe. The latter, opened in 1887, was Bournemouth's main hospital until the Royal Bournemouth opened off Castle Lane in 1992. It was a lengthy journey either way though from 1866 Salisbury could be reached very easily by train. Boscombe was more problematical as the train from Verwood ran into Bournemouth West whilst the bus wound through West Moors, Ferndown, Longham, Bear Cross, Kinson, Winton, Lansdowne to Bournemouth where one changed for Boscombe. Neither is easy by public transport today!

Friendly Societies such as the Church Benefit Society, Oddfellows and Foresters as well as other "Sick Clubs" took weekly payments as an insurance against the expense of medical treatment. Miss Nora Joy recalled that she was lucky or unlucky enough to require hospitalisation on the very week that the payments to date enabled her to qualify. "Hospital Sundays" with processions and events were organised to raise funds.

As described, the Church School log books reveal a catalogue of diseases, then serious and often fatal. After Dr. Vann, his successors called regularly to vaccinate children but no other routine medical checks were made at the school until the twentieth century.

SICKNESS AND HEALTH

In 1913 Dr. Manning made a Medical Inspection whilst in May 1923 a Health Visitor, Miss Mountbatten of Shillingstone, visited the school. Dental Inspections are not recorded until the same year. A designated School Nurse is not mentioned until 1931. It was not until 1921 that Dr. Charles Girling opened a surgery at the Restynge House in Ringwood Road. He lived in a large, old house named "Chaseborough" (Thomas Hardy's name for Cranborne) in Dewlands Way. The house has recently been demolished and together with the large walled garden is now the site of blocks of flats. Amongst other duties, Dr. Girling carried out regular checks on the workers at the Crossroads Pottery under the Factory and Workshop Acts 1901 – 1911 including the fitness of young persons and children for employment.

In the early years of the twentieth century the only Nurse in Verwood was the unqualified "Sister Hannah" who lived in Ringwood Road and attended mainly at births and deaths. On being called out she first had to catch her pony and then harness it to a trap. Apparently she was not too pleased when an official District Nurse with a more easily manageable bicycle was appointed. Two sisters who had qualified at Plaistow Training Hospital, London arrived on the Dorset scene. Nurse May Armstrong came around 1930 to Cranborne from where she was expected to cover by bicycle an area including Wimborne St. Giles, the Gussages and Verwood. Her sister Lillian followed and first worked as a mental nurse at Herrison Hospital, Dorchester but was also qualified in general and dental nursing and midwifery. Due to an increase of population, Dr. Clarke of Cranborne invited Lillian to cover the Verwood part of her sister's area. Working together, the sisters were able to call on each other's expertise. One night they were summoned at 8 p.m. to attend a gypsy in labour. They searched Handley Down all night but were unable to find the camp. They came across a shepherd who told them that some of his hurdles had been used as a shelter. This they found at 7 a.m. between the ancient burial mounds on Handley Down. They crawled in and Lillian delivered the baby. Crawling out again they were met by six bright-eyed children who were promptly checked over by May.

Lillian, pictured left, married a Verwood man, Evan Ziph Brewer, in 1934 and although most married women had to give up their career, she was asked to stay on which she did until expecting her daughter Hillary late the following year. Although Nurse Constance Duffet was appointed to take over her duties, Lillian was still called upon, taking in foster children and maternity cases in her own home as well as supplementary nursing around the village. On one occasion the doctor called at 11 p.m. to ask her to take in a family of six children found abandoned in a ditch which she did until alternative accommodation could be found. During the terrifying night of 23rd/24th April 1944 she was called out to the death of Max Barrett in Hillside Road and then on to a woman injured by shrapnel at Ebblake. She was sent an escort of four burly Home Guard personnel whom she declared she could well manage without but who religiously stuck to their duty. As her husband was serving in the Royal Navy and seconded to a training post in the United States, she had to leave the young but capable Hillary under the dining table with the ration books, valuables and a foster child to mind. She had been helping her mother wash babies since the age of 7.

From the mid twentieth century, the sick, injured and expectant mothers of Verwood and Three Legged Cross were looked after by District Nurses of the Verwood and Three Cross Nursing Association. In 1944 it was reported at the parish meeting that 3771 visits had been made. Subscribers to the association had increased by 41 to 321 and there had also been a flag day and donations. Constance Duffett was also a greatly loved District Nurse who ministered to Verwood until the early 1960s when Nurse Mary Fuller took over. At the Parish Council meeting in 1944 it was agreed to send a letter of thanks to Nurse Duffett and her mother. At the 1945 meeting the Chairman declared Nurse Duffett to be the kindest person who ever entered a working man's home.

SICKNESS AND HEALTH

POST WAR HEALTH VISITING

These notes were written in 1976 by Health Visitor Nurse Mary Fuller, pictured on her rounds, recalling nearly thirty years experience in Verwood and the surrounding district. They give an illuminating account of the conditions of the time.

"Until 1948 Health Visitors were responsible for the health and welfare of all children under the age of 5 years in their geographical area. This also included children who were placed for adoption and foster children. The Health Visitor often acted as Third Party in adoption transactions.

The Health Visitor was also the School Nurse and carried out regular cleanliness inspections having the statutory right to take action where necessary. As a rule she was able to gain the parents' co-operation.

The Health Visitor was also the T.B. nurse which meant visiting the patients regularly, mainly to ensure that contacts were checked up, i.e. X-rayed etc. and that there was no risk of infection spreading if the T.B. was active. Usually domiciliary patients had quiescent T.B., having had either surgery or drugs. It was also possible to obtain extra milk allowances for them and a shelter was provided for the garden, which was suitable for sleeping, if necessary.

When I started health visiting in 1948, I had a case load of approximately 550 under fives, 11 schools and approximately 60 T.B. patients. Due to the N.H.S. 1948 Act, more Health Visitors were appointed, as we then became responsible for the welfare of the elderly – over 60s in the area and also all physically handicapped patients and more procedures had to be carried out in the Schools. This included attending all medical inspections with the Medical Officer of Health in the schools in the area, twice yearly; testing sight and measuring weight; giving polio vaccinations and deaf testing. Latterly these procedures were carried out on the school entrants. They were very time consuming and meant several visits to the schools and often to the homes.

Cleanliness inspections still had to be carried out, although there was a long period for several years in the 1960s when it was seldom necessary as the modern treatments practically eradicated the head louse! Unfortunately by the 70s it reared its ugly head again becoming resistant to the lotions.

Health Visitors were not responsible for fostered or adopted children after 1948 as the Children's Act was passed and a Children's Department and Officers were entirely responsible for thse children. Then later this work was taken over by the Social Services and by the late 60s they had also appointed social workers to be responsible for the elderly and physically handicapped. We worked closely with the social workers and had regular conferences to discuss problem families and especially latterly "battered babies" or injuries of unknown origin.

We did not begin to liaise with G.P.s until the sixties, which was not really very satisfactory at first. All reports, returns and records were sent to Dorchester County Hall Health Department and the G.Ps were contacted from there if necessary. Gradually the G.P. attachment developed, in readiness for April 1974.

Health Visitors still had to visit the elderly in the area and report to Social Services to take action if necessary. It was not necessary when District Nurses were also calling.

The case loads remained about the same. Sometimes they were adjusted by County Hall if too heavy or too light (which was seldom!).

I had only 5 T.B. patients by 1975 but the numbers were replaced by approximately 150 elderly which had gradually increased through the years. This was one great advantage of working with G.P.s, having access to records of elderly, who needed visiting.

SICKNESS AND HEALTH

The Child Welfare Clinic in Verwood was opened during the Second World War years. Previous to this, Ferndown was the nearest Clinic to which free transport was sent. There was an influx of refugees here and there was a demand for one. National Dried Milk at 10d a tin, orange juice at 5d a bottle and cod liver oil free of charge were issued from the clinics and also cheap Marmite, Virol and vitamin drops and other brands of dried milk as they came on the market. Voluntary workers ran the clinics but a Health Visitor and a Doctor (M.O.H.) who gave all prophyliaxis treatments including smallpox vaccinations were always present. If a child was found to have a defect or ailment it was referred to the G.P.

During the early 1950s the clinics were very hectic as there was a severe polio epidemic in the area and as the vaccine was given by injection then the M.O.H. was responsible. Then the vaccine was offered to adults and special polio clinics were opened in the village halls in all the surrounding villages to cope with the demand. These clinics were opened in the evenings as well for the workers. Gradually the clinics were discontinued as the epidemic abated.

When the Secondary Modern School at Cranborne was opened, the Headmaster asked for Health Education to be given by the Health Visitor to girls of 14. Consent had to be obtained from the girls' parents as the course included more intimate subjects such as puberty, conception, development and birth of a baby, V.D. etc. The course lasted three months and was given for seven years until the Middle School developed at Cranborne for younger children.

This followed classes given for expectant mothers including health education talks and relaxation exercises. Demonstrations were also given. Nurses, Midwives and Health Visitors ran these classes regularly for fifteen years.

My area covered one of the most rural parts of Dorset and one spent a great deal of one's time travelling around the villages which were as far away as Tarrant Gunville, Chettle, Woodcutts, East and West Woodyates including Sixpenny Handley, the two Crichels, two Gussages, Horton, Three Cross, Woodlands, Cranborne, Alderholt and Verwood as well as several hamlets and scattered farmsteads. The Doctor at Handley discovered that his practice covered 500 square miles, so mine must have covered 1000 square miles!!

I am very glad to know that now there are many more workers in the field to enable the Health Visitor to give her expertise and time to the work for which she was trained. I understand that help is also given for Health Visitor's clerical work now. As hours of one's time was spent keeping records and writing reports as well as phoning and attending meetings, conferences and refresher courses, I think this is really necessary."

In earlier days mothers usually gave birth in their own home or sometimes for a first baby at their parents' house where they could be in the comforting circumstances of having their mother present. In later years "Kersbrook" was once a little maternity home in Church Road, Three Legged Cross run by Mrs. Woods. Up to the late 1970s many Verwood babies were born at Fordingbridge Cottage Hospital just over the border in Hampshire and therefore have the "wrong county" on their birth certificates as opposed to their parental home.

One of the best remembered of Verwood General Practitioners was Dr. Havelock Pearson who held his surgery in a downstairs room of the semi detached house in Vicarage Road, now the H.S.B.C., until about 1960 then at a house on the west wide of Manor Road near to the Crossroads. There was no appointment system so patients just turned up and sat "patiently" waiting sometimes for hours as the doctor believed in giving his full attention to whatever the current visitor was complaining of, often relieving symptoms just by chatting over interesting subjects. This is a luxury practitioners can no longer afford but neither would most people be prepared for such a long wait. This surgery then transferred to larger premises at another converted house "Elim" on the corner of Church Hill and Manor Road, which was formerly the home of Mr. Edwin Morey, quarry proprietor, and is now the site of Church Hill Court. In 2000 it moved to a purpose built block in Station Road. Cranborne doctors also have a practice in Lake Road and West Moors doctors at Three Legged Cross.

TRANSPORT

ROADS

From time immemorial the only alternative to "Shank's Pony" had been the horse, either ridden or pulling a carriage or cart. Folk thought little of walking several miles each day to work or on other business. The carrier's cart provided an alternative means of economically moving people and goods. A conveyance ran from Verwood Station to Cranborne twice daily in the late nineteenth century but this was probably more for the convenience of the outlying folk than those of Verwood itself. Apart from the turnpike road through Three Legged Cross there were no official main thoroughfares and no coaching inns for passengers' accommodation. It was just a place to be passed through en route to somewhere else.

Towards the end of the nineteenth century the invention of the combustion engine was about to change all that. At first motorized vehicles were well outside the price range of ordinary folk and the horse was still "King of the Road" but as time and inevitability wore on the changeover was made. Motor cars were looked on as a wonderful rarity and able to command central position on the almost deserted roads.

*A solitary car in an almost deserted Ringwood Road. The shop on the right was Mr. Legg's
then Dan Andrews', Butchers, and is currently a restaurant*

Inevitably one of these icons was owned by Squire Fryer who promoted his Gardener, Oliver Thorne, to the rank of Chauffeur at least on a part time basis. Apparently Oliver made a habit of putting too much oil in the engine and so acquired the nickname "All A Fire".

As no Driving Test was required until 1935 people either taught themselves or learned from those with a little more experience. Miss Gertrude Sims recalled that on driving to Ringwood, when the hills were much sharper than they are today, she would pull into the side of the road on seeing a car approach from the opposite direction and wait for it to pass before continuing on her way. She said that in 1921 there were only four cars in Verwood, owned by herself, Job Brewer, the Vicar of Woodlands and Vince Parker who ran a taxi service.

TRANSPORT

Some fathers whose business depended on horse transport handed the figurative reins over to their sons when this new fangled method was introduced. One old chap at least is known to have called out "Whoaa" and pulled on the steering wheel every time he applied the brakes. Another would never shut the car door until the engine was well and truly started as he was afraid that if it caught fire he would not get out in time. Gradually though the horse was phased out as car and lorry transport took over. Motors of whatever shape or form were doubtless very exciting to the younger generation and required no extra attention such as feeding and grooming once parked in the garage. They probably also saved many young arms from aching as one of the traditional if hated chores of the youth had been to chop gorse collected off the common in a hand turned machine until the horse's fodder appeared at the other end. As the horse ate, so the process had to be repeated. The welfare of the horse was of paramount importance to a family's fortunes.

The early 20th Century Bus Service which called at Three Legged Cross
From the festive nature of the passengers' costumes it was probably
either the inaugural journey or a special local occasion

Three Legged Cross had had its own early bus service on a circular route which ran from Bournemouth twice daily taking in Ensbury, Kinson, Longham, Ferndown, West Moors, Three Cross, Horton Heath, Wigbeth, Horton, Horton Inn, Highlea, Stanbridge, Wimborne, Corfe Mullen, Canford, Kinson and Winton. It also had a commercial deck for milk churns and goods. The journey must have taken hours with solid tyres bumping over unmade roads and been a penance for the passengers on the upper deck in bad weather.

Motor charabancs appeared to augment the recreational travel already available by then on the railway and these were eagerly hired for the traditional once a year day trip to the seaside, Weymouth being a popular destination.

In the 1930s Verwood Parish Council repeatedly wrote to the Hants & Dorset Bus Company asking them to improve services, a) By running a bus from Ringwood to Verwood through Ashley Heath: b) By improving the early morning and late night services. Predictably the company dallied over these until in the end they could declare "There is a War on" so nothing could be done about it.

TRANSPORT

In 1944 the company was requested to run a direct bus from Verwood to Bournemouth through West Moors to save having to change at Ferndown. In the late 1940s the bus route to Bournemouth ran through Three Legged Cross, West Moors, Ferndown (changing for Wimborne), Longham, Kinson, and Winton. To get to the hospital in Boscombe you had to change buses at the Lansdowne. The A338 "Spur Road" was not built until the early 1970s.

Edward Hastings "Ted" Saunders started "Sunflower" motor coaches at Ebblake after the First World War. He had two buses and a taxi and also for a short while a lorry. In the 1980s a private company "Verwood Transport" filled a gap in the routes of the major companies. Children remembered their journey to Upper School at Wimborne on board the blue painted Routemaster bus.

At the Parish Council Meeting of 24th April 1939, the subject of the dangerous nature of Verwood Crossroads had been raised together with that at the junction of Vicarage and Ringwood Roads. After considerable discussion it was unanimously agreed, on the proposition of Mr. Cannell, that representation should be made to Dorset County Council for the erection of a "Halt" sign on the Vicarage Road approach to Ringwood Road and "Flow" signs on the Manor and Edmondsham Road approaches to the Ringwood-Station Road. It is ironic that the 2006 County Council's attempt to redress this problem to meet the exigencies of the present age has been met with nothing like universal approval in the community.

Shearing's Cycle and Motor Cycle Repairs at Verwood Crossroads

At around the same time as the motor vehicle was invented but much more readily available to the general public came the advent of the bicycle. This ingenious machine instantly opened up a whole new world for communications, social activities and employment.

Motor Cycles provided a more affordable alternative to the car as well as thrills for the younger generation.

One branch of the Shearing family found itself competent to move at the speed of the outside world. Joseph Shearing and his son Charles were Blacksmiths in Forge Lane, then on an important entry point to Verwood from Horton. Charles' son Frederick Charles, born 1880 and known as Fred, built a new forge near the south-west corner of the Crossroads, diversifying into cycle and later motor-cycle repairs. Fred also cut hair in the cycle shed at the front, repairs sometimes having to wait until the current barbering was finished. His son Eric, born 1912, then began a motor garage on the site. As well as selling fuel, it had a repair shop and second hand car sales. Later sold to Otton's and then Heynes, it ceased trading and was demolished in 2000, the site becoming Duke's Court flats.

In Ringwood Road "The Nook" garage was owned by Mr. Bates and later by Ron Curd the name changing to "Verwood Motors". Since the early 1980s it has been in the capable hands of former Poole Pirates and England speedway star, Pete Smith and his family. The sales and repair shop are now known as "Verwood Ford" whilst the forecourt fuel sales trades as "Verwood Shell" and is the only fuel station left in Verwood. Others used to be the Manor Road Garage, owned by the Fox family and the Central Garage opposite the Recreation Ground. At Three Legged Cross Richard Gunning sold petrol from a shack until the late 1960s when Mr. & Mrs. Murphy bought the business and transformed it into the modern fuel station we know today.

David Sherred, born 1892 at Three Legged Cross with his bicycle in the early twentieth century, wearing a smart suit, strong leather boots and cycle clips.

A young lady, similarly well attired with her ladies' model. Could she be one of his sisters? At least she must have been a Three Legged Cross girl of the same era.

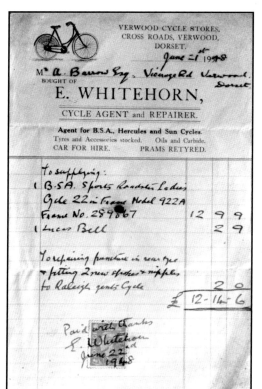

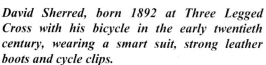

In 1948 a BSA Sports Roadster Lady's bicycle, complete with bell, could be bought from Mr. Whitehorn of the Verwood Cycle Stores for £12.14.6.

With a 50 year Guarantee!!

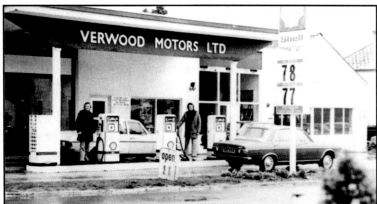

VERWOOD MOTORS IN RINGWOOD ROAD

Filling up on a snowy winter's day in the 1970s. The price in those days was per gallon, not per litre.

MANOR ROAD GARAGE

It stood on the northern corner of Springfield Road opposite Burnbake Road. It has since been demolished and is now the site of "Foxes Court". In the 1930s it was owned by W. Vincent who advertised "Austin and Cowley Saloons for Hire – Any Distance". He must also have been Verwood's first Travel Agent with "Tours arranged for England, Scotland, Wales and the Continent. Itinerary made out and can give the best terms". One wonders how many local folk availed themselves of this offer.

TRANSPORT

RAILWAYS

Verwood was the first Dorset station on the Salisbury and Dorset Junction Railway which linked Salisbury to Poole, the line opening on 20th December 1866. The village therefore had a station well before Bournemouth where West Station was built in 1874 and Bournemouth Central not until 1885. Long before the establishment of Bournemouth as a holiday resort, Poole had always been the commercial hub on this part of the south coast. The line was taken over by London & South Western Railway, the old L.S.W.R., in 1883 and remained in their hands until passing to Southern Railway in 1923. Under nationalization it became part of British Railways from 1948 until its closure. The line was single track except through the stations with a "tablet" being handed over to ensure that no two trains were on the same stretch at the same time.

From the moment the station opened, Verwood came into its own. Business flourished and the goods of the area, vegetables, milk, watercress from Wimborne St. Giles and Cranborne, together with pottery, were able to be exported much further afield than had previously been the case with a horse and cart. Earthenware dealers doubled their trade by sending ahead one wagon load, taking a full cart in the direction of the train then replenishing their stock at the selected station when the first batch of goods had been sold. Sand was exported to South Wales for use in the glass making and brick industries from 1906 onwards. Items such as coal and roofing slates were brought into the village and, ironically, lighter, enamelled household goods which were to contribute to the decline of the native potteries.

Looking north towards Salisbury with Verwood station and track staff

The railway also opened up new horizons, bringing people who had been born well outside the county with tales of their own to tell. Conversely, several young Verwood men obtained work on the railways and moved further afield. Some brought children back to Verwood to be christened amongst family and friends. Thus we learn that around 1873 Seth Bennett had obtained employment as a Railway Gatekeeper and Signalman in Surrey. He and his wife, Keturah Ann (Kate) née Orman returned from Godalming and later Woking for the baptism of their younger offspring.

Conversely, George Guy came from Piddlehinton to be a Railway Porter at Verwood Station and married a local girl, Emily Budden. They lived in a cottage in Does Lane having twelve children, some of whom became ancestors of several village families whilst one son, Dudley Frank, emigrated to Canada and joined the Royal Mounted Police.

Several men, however, welcomed the change in employment offered on a local basis as opposed to the inevitable agricultural labouring of their forebears. The Davis and Jacobs families of Three Legged Cross in particular embraced this new technology with employment as Railway Platelayers, Linesmen and Gatekeepers. Sadly, two elderly men with long experience, Thomas Davis and Mark Jacobs, were killed on the Ringwood to Wimborne line south of Woolsbridge on Wednesday 8th March 1893 and lie buried in Verwood churchyard. They were working on their length at 7.30 on a very foggy morning and when they saw the up train approaching they stepped into the other track without hearing or seeing that a ballast train was coming with predictably fatal results.

Looking south from the railway bridge on the Verwood to Cranborne Road.

The chimneys of Verwood and Gotham Brick Works rise in the background.

An engine is shunting in the sidings of the Station Yard.

The station yard became a busy, bustling place. The brickyard built a siding onto the line and one of the best remembered of businesses sited there was "Dorset Farmers", a co-operative dealing in agricultural supplies. At least four local men, Tom Steele, Ira Henning, Lot Budden and Valentine Reeks became Coal Merchants. Wood and turf, available for free on the commons, had been the staple fuel over the centuries but for a moderate charge the coal delivery removed the necessity of all the labour involved.

As the nearest station to the great houses of Cranborne, Wimborne St. Giles and Crichel, royalty and other eminent personages were frequent visitors. In the 1940s the Station Master kept his little girl at home from school without giving her a reason. Later he took her onto the platform and through the train window she saw King George VI and Queen Elizabeth, an impression which remained with her vividly.

Alongside these were the many thousands of ordinary passengers over the years and the village was devastated when the line was marked as superfluous under the Beeching Axe. It closed to passengers on 2nd May 1964 and to goods the following year. The only reminders of the station's existence now are the Albion Hotel and the old railway arches in Station Road, Edmondsham Road and Horton Way. The course of the line through Verwood has become totally overgrown. Three Legged Cross did not have a station as the trains ran right through to West Moors under a railway arch in Horton Road near the present Village Hall.

A steam engine approaches, pulling the train en route from Salisbury to Poole

The original stations on this line were Salisbury, Downton, Breamore, Fordingbridge, Daggons Road (for Alderholt, a name chosen to avoid confusion with Aldershot), Verwood and West Moors where there was a junction with the line coming in from London via the New Forest and Ringwood. Thereafter it continued to Wimborne, Broadstone and Poole Junction (later Hamworthy Junction), followed by a continuation to Poole town, Parkstone, Branksome and Bournemouth West. Creekmoor was added south of Broadstone in 1933 to serve an adjacent munitions factory.

Engine No. 31792 with a train for Salisbury arriving at Verwood on 11th April 1964, less than a month before the passenger service ended. By this time the familiar Station Brickwork chimneys had been demolished.

Above: Mr. Ira Henning, Coal Merchant left, Bob the Stationmaster's dog and Mr. George Eyres on Verwood Station in the 1930s.
Right: Bob helpfully puts in a stint as relief Porter!

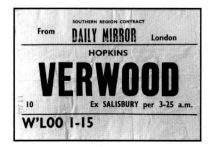

Above: A label directing the delivery of the Daily Mirror to Hopkins Newsagency to be sent to Verwood Station from Waterloo via Salisbury.

Right: Verwood Station paralysed in an exceptionally snowy winter.

From Three Legged Cross railway bridge, since demolished, looking south at the single track running towards West Moors.

The Horton Road rose sharply to cross over the line. Those driving north to the junction from West Moors had no vision whatsoever of any traffic coming over the hill from the left of the road.

FARMING AND SMALLHOLDING

There would have been farms along the fertile valley of the River Crane for centuries. In 1377 William de Bello Bosco (William of Fairwood) mentions, amongst his property, his meadows and pastures. It is unlikely that such a prominent local landowner's holdings would not have encompassed some of them at least. The farms probably stood on pre-Conquest sites dating back to time immemorial, being rebuilt and restructured as architecture and farming practices changed and wealth grew.

There were ten farms in and around Verwood on the Crane Valley from north to south: Westworth, East and West Farms (previously Lower Farm) at Romford, Bridge Farm, Verwood Farm, Verwood Manor Farm, Potterne, Kings, Woolsbridge Manor and Woolsbridge. Some of the farm names have been interchangeable at some stages as can be witnessed on maps. Verwood Manor has been called Verwood Farm. Woolsbridge is particularly confusing as two farms are sometimes called just Woolsbridge Farm. Some of these whose farmhouses are in other parishes have lands lying within Verwood or Cranborne parish as it was until 1886. Potterne Farm is mentioned in documents as early as the 13th century and Romford Mill and Manor Farm, then known as Cray's Manor, are well documented in the 1600s.

Verwood Farm – Home of William Standfield and family
One of the few farmhouses to remain thatched

Until the end of the 19th century, agriculture dominated the life of Verwood and the farms were the major source of employment for the men. Towards the end, the industry started to decline though there was still much farming activity well into the 20th century. Mechanical farm equipment reduced the need for the labour of both men and horses whilst opportunities arose for the men to go into other trades.

FARMING AND SMALLHOLDING

The lure of cities such as London and the availability of employment there started to break the pattern of continuous living in the home parish but Verwood was unusual, for an agricultural area, in increasing its population over the nineteenth century. Many Verwood families can still be traced through from the earliest recorded days and their descendants still live in and around the area. Others decided to emigrate or had the decision taken for them as in the case of the Andrews brothers, John and James, Verwood farm labourers, convicted at Dorchester in 1827 for poaching and sentenced to seven years transportation. They landed in Van Diemen's Land (Tasmania) aboard the "Bengal Merchant" but later moved to mainland Victoria where they married, lived long lives and became well respected, prosperous citizens. Their brother Joseph who, according to a descendant, was allegedly as guilty as they but not caught, remained in Verwood in the usual everyday existence of those times.

The term "Ag Lab" or agricultural labourer seems to imply one of the lower orders and indeed they were never well paid. However, the term covered a multitude of skills and experience in animal husbandry, crop growing, hedge laying, weather forecasting and the like without which a farm could not be efficiently run. The ploughman was out all day with only his horses for company and his own pride in the straightness and neatness of his furrows. There was land to spare in Verwood for each family to have a cottage garden and after a long day toiling in the fields the men would often be up half the night, sometimes by lamplight, tending these and still be ready to wake early the next morning for work. Women and children were often pressed into service at busy seasons of the year such as planting, sowing, haymaking and harvesting.

Does Hatches on the River Crane, one of a series of sluice gates controlling the Water Meadow system
The river formed a natural pool here which became a favourite bathing and picnic spot

The Crane Valley farms were linked to form a Water Meadow system. This allowed a gentle stream of river water to pass over the fields, protecting the growing grass from frost and encouraging its early growth for pasturing. The water was not allowed to lie stagnant but controlled by a series of hatches, sluices and channels to promote a continuous flow. Downstream from Romford the control gates were named Webb's Hole after a magistrate who had fishing rights, Does Hatches and Iron Hatches on the boundary of West Farm and Bridge Farm.

FARMING AND SMALLHOLDING

The fields were flooded for about ten weeks after Christmas and great co-operation was needed amongst the farmers to open and close the gates at the right time to allow the water onto the next farm.

The pasture was used for grazing cattle as it was too wet for sheep. At one time a Lord Shaftesbury insisted on putting sheep on his water meadows despite the advice of his tenant farmers and workers. Needless to say, the unfortunate sheep contracted foot rot and liver fluke so the experiment was not repeated. The Wimborne St. Giles Estate, Lord Shaftesbury's seat, owned much land in this part of Verwood and installed the hatch system.

In contrast to the fertile valley of the Crane and the chalk downlands of Cranborne Chase which supported many sheep, the clay soils of Verwood gave way to much small scale agriculture. The land was not highly valued by the Landowners who often owned vast tracts; The Earl of Normanton of Somerley to the north and east; The Marquess of Salisbury of Hatfield House and Cranborne Manor to the north-west; the Earl of Shaftesbury of Wimborne St. Giles to the west and Squire William Rolles Fryer of Wimborne and Lytchett Minster to the south. Where their lands met, large boundary stones were placed with their initials or other insignia.

The Tithe Map and Apportionment of 1847 is our first overall introduction to land ownership, occupancy and use in Verwood. Tithes had been paid in kind from produce, animals or poultry. It was decided to commute this unwieldy system into cash payments so for this purpose all the land on which tithes were due was assessed. The tithes due in Horton and Woodlands had been similarly valued earlier in 1841.

The farmhouse of West Farm, Romford, previously Lower Farm, built of brick and tiled
William James, son of William Standfield farmed here in the late 19th and early 20th centuries

Unfortunately for the knowledge of Verwood, much of the land in the then Cranborne Parish belonging to Eastworth, Burrows and Verwood Farm was already tithe free so no information is given. This is true also for the land east of Romford almost as far as today's Manor Road and south to the parish boundary.

FARMING AND SMALLHOLDING

Fortunately, another schedule exists from 1867 when W. H. Hewitt was selling land which shows that in addition to Eastworth and Burrows Farms, there was also a large, separate holding to the north of Eastworth Road with fields to the south of it. This was farmed at that time by Richard Standfield, one of the three brothers from Tolpuddle who leased and later owned land around the parish.

The Verwood Tithe Apportionment shows the largest recorded farms to be Potterne Farm of about 283 acres, farmed by Henry Duell for Lady Bingham, and Verwood Manor Farm of some 130 acres, farmed by Joseph Gallop for William Fryer. The largest private farm was Woolsbridge Manor owned and farmed by Ambrose Witt with a recorded acreage of 76 though some fields belonging to the farm may have been in the parish of St. Leonards and St. Ives. Thomas Bluton held 57 acres from the Earl of Normanton on the land where Morrison's supermarket now stands which included Bugden's Copse. This land was owned in later years by a branch of the Thorne family.

The rest were smallholdings of a few acres and cottage gardens where a few chickens or pigs could be kept and vegetables cultivated. Where the land had not been naturally fertile the succession of livestock added their own nutrients over the years. There was always sufficient room in Verwood to grow home produce as there was not the pressing need for land as in more agriculturally productive areas. In Three Legged Cross particularly the land was given over to market gardening.

Mr. Frederick Arthur Poolman outside his cottage at Westworth.
Cottagers could make use of the large gardens to provide food for their families and sometimes for sale.
Progress of crops provided a common talking point amongst the men

WESTWORTH is in the parish of Edmondsham but its lands reached right down to Eastworth with which in mediaeval days it was known by the name of "Horsych". This settlement was then a Manor, quite separate from Verwood itself. In 1867 it was farmed by William Sweatman and contained arable land, pasture, woods, meadows and an orchard as well as a withy or reed bed.

Westworth Farm itself is hidden from the road on a track to the left of the road to Alderholt but a farm cottage belonging to the Estate was situated on the right of the road. For many years it was occupied by Mr. Frederick Arthur Poolman whose prize vegetables were regular winners at Verwood Horticultural Show. His son Frank said knowingly that he was a carter and had access to manure! Afterwards the cottage stood derelict until it was completely restored and rebuilt into a luxury home. Westworth Farm itself has in recent years undergone extensive restoration and reconstruction resulting in the addition of new homes on the site.

EAST FARM, ROMFORD lies to the north of the Verwood to Cranborne Road, just inside Edmondsham parish. Its outward appearance conceals vestiges of a much earlier construction with timber framing inside a small back room corresponding to a chimney outside where new brick surrounds the old. The roof inside the bedroom is wattle hurdle daubed with mud.

A pastoral view over Romford on the western fringe of Verwood parish

In the 1830s to 1850s it was farmed by Robert Standfield, first father then son of the same name who continued until his death in 1857. Thereafter the tenancy passed in an interesting manner to George Ingram whose sister Jane had married William Standfield of Verwood Farm. Another sister, Ann, was later to marry Richard Standfield. Yet another sister Elizabeth had married Henry Andrews of Sandalholme pottery who was first cousin to George's second wife, Leah Bailey of the Moor Lodge pottery. These families are described in the section dealing with Verwood potteries. That the families were close knit is borne out by the fact that George and Leah are buried next to William and Jane in Verwood Churchyard. However, like their father Aaron who had worked at Verwood Farm, George never aspired to being a farmer remaining at various times a shepherd, agricultural labourer and carter. In 1881 he was acting in the latter capacity to the farmer Thomas Coombs. By 1891 Frank Standfield, one of William's sons, was farming the East property assisted by an "Ag Lab" George James Ingram, son of George and Leah and therefore his first cousin. George James had shifted his mode of employment by 1901 when he was working as a carter in the brickyard. This may have had something to do with the fact that his sister Emma Jane was married to the Brick Manufacturer and builder, Job Brewer, whose name occurs many times in Verwood's history.

By this date East Farm had passed to Frederick J. Luscombe, who is remembered as keeping racehorses there in the early twentieth century. In 1911 Charles and Mary Anne Reeks moved with their family from Sutton Holmes and in later years two of their sons, Tony and Bertie, worked the land. On their retirement in 1972 the Frouds of West Farm, just over the road, took over the farm tenancy and the Waterfield family came to live in the house.

FARMING AND SMALLHOLDING

LOWER FARM, now West Farm Romford, lies to the south of the Cranborne Road. Its lower fields encompassed the water meadows of the River Crane whilst its upper fields rose towards the chalk of Cranborne Chase. Like many other Estate farmhouses it was built of brick in a time when ordinary Verwood cottages were cob "mudwall" structures. The Shaftesbury Estate had its own brickyard. Although the house is in Wimborne St. Giles parish, its fields extended into Woodlands, Horton and Edmondsham.

William James Standfield (son of William of Verwood Farm) was the farmer here in the late 19th century and after him came the Lush family before it came into the possession of the Frouds who still remain. Much of the original holding is now Crane Valley Golf Course whilst farm buildings have been converted into attractive Holiday Lodges.

VERWOOD FARM and **BRIDGE FARM**. Verwood Farm which lies off Margards Lane, had extensive acreage and was held by William Standfield from the Earl of Shaftesbury for much of the 19th century. The land William farmed at various times, according to the census returns, varied between 200 and 340 acres. The Horton Tithe Apportionment of 1841 shows that a substantial proportion of these were water meadows.

The farmhouse, now completely rebuilt following a fire in 1985, was of very ancient construction containing cob, lath and plaster with beams, narrow passageways and sloping floors in the upper rooms . Unlike the other farmhouses, it remained thatched throughout its existence. There was a dairy house attached which still remains as a separate cottage. On the opposite side of the track stood a very extensive square farmyard with barns, stables and cattle sheds but these collapsed a few years ago. By then the property had been bought by Dorset County Council with a view to the site of a new school.

The farmhouse was in Verwood parish but its lands extended westward into Horton parish to what is now Bridge Farm on Horton Way. The 1841 Tithe Map for Horton shows a house, garden, buildings and yards where Bridge Farm is today but these were presumably used by William Standfield to house one of his key farm workers and to provide a base at the far end of his property. In his will William describes himself "of Verwood Bridge Farm in Cranborne parish" so it appears he used the names of both farms as we know them today but lived in the Verwood farmhouse.

A boundary stone, found in a ditch, marked the transition to land held by William Rolles Fryer who owned Verwood Manor Farm to the south and east. William's sons continued at the farm and also at Hayward's Farm on the opposite side of Margards Lane. Verwood's early home cricket pitch was in one of its fields and some are now the playing fields for Emmanuel Middle School. Bridge Farm retains its isolated, rural location.

VERWOOD MANOR FARM is the first farm on the River Crane, wholly within Verwood parish. It lies down St. Michael's Road and is bounded on the west by Verwood Farm and on the east by Potterne Farm. Like other important Farmhouses in the area it was probably built in the late Eighteenth Century on a much earlier foundation. It was previously known as "Cray's Manor" from Jeremiah Cray who lived here in earlier days.

In 1847 it was held by Joseph Gallop for the owner, William Rolles Fryer and consisted of just over 130 acres. However, Joseph Gallop was not in Verwood on the 1841 census though his son-in-law Charles Elmes and his family were. The inference is that Charles Elmes was farming it for him as by 1851 he had taken over the farm and his widowed mother-in-law, Ann Gallop was living with them. Tenants and managers then changed in quick succession so that in 1861 we see Samuel Crumpler, 1871 George Ford and 1881 Charles Lucas. The acreage varied between 167 and 200.

Towards the end of the century it was farmed by Sam Thorne, a local man, and became more of a settled family home. He was the son of the farm gamekeeper and grew up in the keeper's cottage in Crab Orchard Way. He was married to Louise Chamberlin, daughter of the Congregational Pastor, Samuel Thomas.

FARMING AND SMALLHOLDING

POTTERNE FARM was owned on the 1847 Tithe Map by Lady Emma Bingham and occupied by Henry Duell. It then consisted of 283 acres of mixed arable, pasture, meadow, water mead and coppice at a tithe value of £53. As mentioned earlier, Lady Bingham was the widow of General Sir George Ridout Bingham, a hero of the Napoleonic Wars who had died in 1832. Sir George came from the family of that name at Melcombe Bingham, further west, but had inherited the farm through his mother's family, the Ridouts of Deans Leaze near Witchampton. His wife Emma was a Pleydell of Whatcombe Manor at Winterborne Clenston whilst her sister Louisa married John Mansel, a fellow officer of Sir George, and inherited another family seat at Smedmore House, Kimmeridge. Louisa was the mother of John Clavell Mansel-Pleydell the noted antiquarian and founder member of the Dorset Natural History and Antiquarian Field Club who in turn inherited Whatcombe House.

After Henry Duell came a succession of tenants or lessees until on Emma's death in 1874 it was acquired by the 3rd Earl of Normanton in whose family it remained until 1920 when much of their estate was being sold. East Dorset District Council purchased the farm land in 1988 for the benefit of the growing community. It is now known as Potterne Park and is home to Verwood's sports and recreational facilities, though the farmhouse remains in private hands.

Potterne Park Sports and Recreational Area, once the fields of Potterne Farm
Scene of the annual Rustic Fayre now organized by Verwood Rotary Club

WOOLSBRIDGE MANOR FARM, sometimes shown as Woolsbridge Farm, whose lands followed on south of Potterne Farm, was unique in being owner occupied. It stretched to the north side of Ringwood Road at Three Legged Cross and was bounded on the west by the vast, uncultivated 779 acreage of the South or Lower Common. In 1847 it occupied 76 acres in Verwood parish but may have extended across the boundary. On the 1851 census it appears that the farmer, Ambrose Witt, declares that he has 911 acres and employs 4 men. This is a huge jump unless he had meanwhile acquired the rights of Lower Common.

Ambrose's father of the same name who died in 1824 "of Woolsbridge" was evidently a wealthy man leaving various estates in Dorset and Hampshire amongst his children. Ambrose himself was born at Harbridge, fairly close by, in the next county.

He married three times and dying in 1855 at the age of 87 was buried in Verwood churchyard. He also owned land in other parts of Verwood parish which he leased to other villagers. His daughter Fanny married Stephen Andrews of Pond Farm on Church Hill, Verwood and their son Dan was assisting his grandfather at Woolsbridge in 1851. His son James was also a fairly substantial farmer in the Three Legged Cross area though the names of the holdings are not always specified on the census. It appears that James had only daughters and so there was no-one to follow on the farming business. His nephew, Dan Ambrose Witt Andrews, carried on at Pond Farm after his parents.

There were several other farms in Verwood, away from the River Crane. In the north of the parish were Eastworth Farm and Burrows Farm. Others were Aggis Farm and Bakers Farm off Station Road, Starlight Farm in St. Stephen's Lane, Hainault Farm and Claylake Farm off Newtown Road and Hayward's Farm off Margards Lane to give some examples. Many of their fields now lie under housing estates, their only memory being reflected in the names given to the roads. Does Farm now lies on the corner of Dewlands Road and Does Lane but the original farm stood in what is now Crane Valley Golf Course. Pond Farm specialised in growing camomile which was sent for processing in London and often picked by children when they should have been at school.

EASTWORTH FARM also served as the "Heathpoult Inn", the sign, now vanished, depicting a pheasant chick or poult on the heath. The bracket for the Inn sign still remains above one of the doors. There were two front doorways, one for the farmer and family and the other for paying customers with rooms set aside on the ground floor for each. The rear passage was worn smooth by the continual rolling of barrels. Opposite stood an oak tree studded with rings where the patrons could tether their horses. In those dark nights and in an isolated location, the lights of the Inn must have come as a welcome sight to the traveller.

Eastworth Farm is one of the most attractive houses with a fascinating history. The building was probably originally thatched and the roof timbers are hand shaped. Its nucleus is late 18th Century but it has since been much extended particularly at the back. It was primarily a dairy farm with John Short Hayter as the tenant farmer in the early 1800s until his retirement to Burton near Christchurch in the late 1850s.

The house was always used as a marking point for Census Enumerators, lying as it does on the northern fringe of the parish. Edward Hooper is the first known owner of the building which was then in the County of Wiltshire. It was purchased by Henry Brouncker in the 1780s and appeared on a map of 1787. It was probably transferred to the Somerley Estate in 1845 when the first tenancy was given but we know that John Hayter had been the sitting tenant from before that date. After a succession of tenancies it was eventually sold by the Somerley Estate in 1919.

John Hayter, like Ambrose Witt born in Harbridge parish, and his wife Elizabeth Mesher had about ten children though very sadly many of them died in infancy. There are headstones in Verwood Churchyard commemorating them and when their parents died at Christchurch they were brought back to be buried with these children. Other children thrived, grew to adulthood and married. John Hayter was a man of some substance, being one of the Churchwardens chosen to represent Verwood at Cranborne Parish Church. As such he was responsible for implementing the Poor Law, collecting subscriptions from the wealthier inhabitants and deciding which deserving cases should be allowed parish relief.

The Heathpoult Inn lay on the smuggling route inland from the then deserted coves around Bournemouth and Christchurch. Burrows Lane, well shaded and running north, was said to be a favoured route for the cargoes in the late 18th and early 19th centuries during the wars with France. Such niceties escaped the smugglers who carried on a thriving trade with their business partners across the Channel. Tea, silk, tobacco and brandy were some of the commodities brought up by packhorse ponies from the coast. Many otherwise respectable citizens not only turned a blind eye but were active participants.

The house was also home to one of Verwood's very few reported ghosts. He was a fairly regular resident, never seen but heard and his presence felt, albeit as a benign one. Occupants have heard the front door open and close, the stair door opened and footsteps climbing up even when, on investigation, there was no-one else in the house.

The Gamekeeper's Cottage off Burrows Lane on Eastworth Farm land

Trade at the Inn declined dramatically when "The Albion" was opened in the 1860s at the Station. Thereafter it was run just as a farm. Apart from the dairy business there was little point in growing crops. As one farmer put it "why grow wheat for pheasants to eat" and so it also became a "Sporting Farm" rearing pheasants for the shoot. Mr. Alexander, the Keeper, had a cottage off Burrows Lane, where broody hens were used to hatch pheasant eggs.

Eastworth Farmhouse was in a dilapidated state when Fred Sims of Springfield and Manor Roads, son of Robert Sims, potter of Newtown Road, took up the tenancy in the early 20th century. Fred enjoyed "tinkering with houses" though his wife and daughter were initially appalled when shown where they were to live. The water from the well under the kitchen floor was undrinkable and, as Fred sank about ten wells without success, they had to go over the road to a thatched cottage to fetch all their requirements.

Eventually though, Fred restored it as a beautiful family home and bought it and the surrounding land from the Somerley Estate when it was auctioned in 1919. It was lived in by members of his family for many years after his death in 1934, in particular his unmarried daughter Gertrude who acted as accountant for the family firm of Sims Builders which carried on Fred's work. She had a fascinating fund of information about the farm and the general history of the area. One story was about a horse they had with a mind of its own, named Tom. Tom worked out how to undo the bolt of his stable door and then how to release the other horses so that many a time the family was out in their night clothes with lanterns trying to round up the animals from the heath.

Fred also enlarged the narrow track opposite the farm laying the bed on heather which does not rot, cutting away a hilly part and filling in further down. It was originally called Sandy Lane but as there was another road of this name in Verwood it was later changed to Eastworth Road. Fred did this in order to have a shortcut to take his milk to the station. This was Tom's last job of the day after which he flatly refused to do any more work.

The house, which has an interesting old fire insurance plate, and its outbuildings have now been converted into very attractive holiday cottages.

FARMING AND SMALLHOLDING

THREE LEGGED CROSS

There were several other smaller farms and smallholdings in Three Legged Cross, carved out of the commons with the naturally acidic soil improved as time went on. Market Gardening became a thriving industry and many hotels in the growing town of Bournemouth were supplied, the produce taken there by horse and cart.

Stephen Orman held Birch Tree Farm at Crab Orchard from William Fryer in 1847 where he was followed by his son Henry Stephen. Another son, Charles made his home at Holly Tree Farm on the Ringwood Road whilst one of Charles' sons, Stephen, farmed at Cob Cottage in Church Road. Members of the Joy family farmed at Woolsbridge, now the Old Barn Farm Inn, Gundry's Farm down School Lane and Evergreen Farm, now part of the Joy's Estate. There were several intermarriages between these two families, some of whom were already cousins. Strawberry fields between what is now Church Road and Verwood Road were owned by the Crutcher family.

Charles and Priscilla Orman with children and grandchildren at Holly Tree Farm in the early 20th Century

It is said that Charles Orman used to regularly walk the twelve miles or so to Bournemouth and back to court his future wife Priscilla Whiffen. However, in 1861, two years before they married, she was living with her family in Verwood. It may be that she and Charles met here but she subsequently moved to Bournemouth perhaps to work. They made their home at Holly Tree Farm where they brought up their twelve children and lived to see some married with children of their own. They were amongst those who took produce to Bournemouth or "Barne" as they called it. When wet, they had a huge umbrella on the cart which could shelter six people. Charles died on 8th April 1913 and was buried on 12th April in Verwood Churchyard on what would have been their Golden Wedding Anniversary. Priscilla survived another twenty years until the age of 88. Members of the Orman family were very photogenic and posed for a series of postcards demonstrating their various agricultural activities.

Well into living memory, there were always roadside vegetable stalls in Three Legged Cross where people could choose their own produce. Now there is an extensive Garden Centre named after its founder John T. Brown and nurseries such as Holly Hedge and White Veil, the latter originally called "Nil Desperandum".

FARMING AND SMALLHOLDING

THE ORMAN FAMILY AT BIRCH TREE FARM, CRAB ORCHARD

This was the Orman's "ancestral home" so far as Verwood was concerned. Joseph Orman, a broom maker born 1789 at Moor Crichel and his wife Keturah born the same year at Hinton Martell had arrived at Crab Orchard by 1810 when their eldest son Stephen was born. They became the ancestors of the others of the name throughout this area and their children married into many local families. Stephen became a broom maker and farmer, marrying Jean Kail, and having eight children amongst whom were Charles of Holly Tree Farm and Henry Stephen who continued at Birch Tree Farm. Henry's first wife Jane, daughter of James Bailey and Jane Hatch, died in 1881 at the birth of their second daughter. He married again in 1893 to Jane Shephard Guy having a son Henry Stephen Shephard Orman (Harry) in 1901, twenty years younger than his previous sister. Harry also continued to farm at Birch Tree.

STEPHEN ORMAN AND FAMILY AT "COB COTTAGE", CHURCH ROAD

Stephen born 1869 was a son of Charles and Priscilla of Holly Tree Farm. Although a first cousin of Harry Orman of Birch Tree Farm he was thirty-two years older. He married Alice Emily Habgood of Witchampton. Their daughter, also Alice Emily was born in 1899 followed by Edith May in 1901.

95

BEAN PICKING AT THREE LEGGED CROSS

This is another of the series of postcards featuring the Orman family in various agricultural pursuits
Far right is George Orman, son of Charles and Priscilla and far left his wife Emily Rose (Emmie).
Second from right is his sister Sarah. They are assisted by David Sherred whose sister Annie
married George and Sarah's youngest brother Walter James Orman in 1914

THRESHING AT HOLLY TREE FARM, THREE LEGGED CROSS

Robert Thorne's steam engine "King of the Forest"
This photograph records the change from manual to mechanized labour. Such machines toured the farms
on a rotational basis with neighbours turning out to help each others' harvest

FARMING AND SMALLHOLDING

Sid Joy at Gundry's Farm, Three Legged Cross with his horse drawn chain harrow.

He was born 1887, the son of James Joy and his wife Tamar Orman and named Sidney Edward.

Gundry's Farm lay on the south side of Ringwood Road at the top of School Lane with the land backing onto West Moors

Sid Joy, centre, his daughter Nora left and Leslie Tubbs loading the hay cart at Gundry's Farm.

Frederick Cecil (Fred) Wood of Crab Orchard with what looks like a cartload of dung about to improve someone's soil conditions.

He was born in 1891, one of ten children of George Henry Wood and his wife Naomi Shutler. George Henry was originally from Hertfordshire.

Left: One of the Davis brothers, either Mark born 1852 or Sam born 1859, dressed for work on the family smallholding, Holly Cottage, Manor Road, Verwood. His trousers are tied below the knee to prevent rats and other unwelcome creatures from running up his legs. They were amongst the children of Philip Davis, originally from Ringwood, and his wife Deborah née Hatchard of Woolsbridge. Philip worked on the Hatchard's farm before marrying Deborah.

Right: Sharpening a scythe, a centuries old cutting and harvesting tool before mechanical reapers.

PLOUGHING OUT PART OF THE SOUTH OR LOWER COMMON

*The furze covered bank separates the cultivated field from the wilder heathland
of which it was once a part*

THE CRAFTS

Craftsmen were the lifeblood of any community and especially a rural one where manufactured goods were not readily obtained. The workers in clay, wood and metal could fashion implements for common everyday use and co-operation was often needed between them. Their art took much training, either from father to son or by long years' apprenticeship before the boy could call himself a "Master".

The expertise of the Carpenter and Wheelwright was in daily use. The wooden components of ploughshares, tool handles, gates, doors, window frames, wheels, carts and other items too numerous to mention were amongst his routine tasks. He was also usually the Undertaker, fashioning the coffins for the dead and furnishing the bier on which to push them. He chose his trees purposefully, oak, ash, beech or elm, each wood being best fitted to a different use. Members of the Bailey family both at Eastworth and Dewlands Common were amongst the Carpenters throughout several eras of Verwood history.

A Verwood Craftsman. Mr. Albert Andrews of Coopers Lane with hay rakes and brooms

The Blacksmith was another whose skill was constantly needed, for farm, garden and home implements, latches and bolts etc. One of his main occupations was the shoeing of horses, an important task when farming and travel both depended on the animal. The Shearing family worked in Forge Lane for many generations, eventually diversifying into bicycles and a motor garage as previously described. There was another forge in Ringwood Road, Verwood where Mr. Percy Sims was the blacksmith, having begun his apprenticeship in 1912. Billy Dymond had a forge and blacksmith's shop at Three Legged Cross, just down the West Moors Road which had opened in 1926 and was operated by the Dymond brothers in 1939. It continued for many years but was redeveloped as part of Dymewood Road in 1997. A Devon blacksmith, Thomas Dymond, had come to work in this area from just before 1901. Many blacksmiths have now transferred their skills to wrought iron work and the intricacy and perfection of their designs can be seen in several showrooms.

The Thatcher was an important highly skilled worker, not only for roofing and repairing cottages and barns but also to cover and waterproof the innumerable ricks and haystacks around the area. Locally grown wheat straw was the probable material used.

THE CRAFTS

The Thatcher used a combination of liggers (horizontal hazel rods), spars and sways to produce ornamental designs along the roof ridge and chimney. William Bendall was the resident Verwood thatcher from the early years of the 19th century until his death in 1877.

The Hurdle Maker was found in and around the hazel coppices of the district. His steady output provided thousands and thousands of his product needed for sheep folding and lambing pens when the Shepherds stayed out in the open along with their flock. These hurdles were easily portable and manoeuvrable by one man enabling them to be moved around with ease. Taller hurdles were used as fencing panels.

Families could settle around the commons in Verwood without much interference from the landowner or his agent though sometimes a nominal rent was required. With an acre of garden and a business depending on largely free materials, a living of sorts could be made, independent of an outside employer.

The Besom Maker made "Witch's Brooms", a true fruit of the heathland commons. There were many in Verwood, especially at Three Legged Cross where the families Coombes, Golding, Joy, Keith, Knowlton, Orman, Phillips, Revell and Steel formed a close knit group plying this trade which needed very little outlay to make a living. In Verwood, John Haskell, Alfie Sims and Albert Andrews are among the best remembered.

These brooms were made entirely from materials found on the Commons, except for the wire used in later years for holding the bond. This meant that their outlay was minimal, the only equipment needed being a wooden "horse" on which to shape the handles, an iron "kettle" in which to boil the heads, a mallet, rudimentary handle shaping tool and an endless supply of Wellington Boots, at least in the later days. Since these could not have been made in Verwood there must have been a thriving import trade in this footwear for many varied occupations. It is said that the broom makers and their families could plunge their hands into near boiling water without any apparent discomfort or ill effect.

In Three Legged Cross heaps of finished brooms were left by the roadside for collection and payment. Higglers took the brooms along with the pots on their rounds and they were in great demand for household, garden and industrial use over a wide area.

Besom brooms can still be bought at certain garden shops and their manufacture is sometimes demonstrated at Craft Fairs. However, this occupation has long since died out in Verwood, along with the need to make a living from the Commons. In Three Legged Cross F.J. Revell & Sons still pursue occupations connected with timber and live in the same house as their forebears with the broom making shed in the garden. Fred Steele's broom making shed in Ringwood Road has been converted into an attractive thatched cottage but these are all the traces left of an industry once so prevalent around this heathland area.

Broom Makers tended to marry each other's sons and daughters. There was one occasion of a double wedding at Cranborne Parish Church on 18th November 1852. Charles Knowlton married Tabitha Phillips. In the same ceremony, Tabitha's brother Charles Phillips married Ann Knowlton, the first Charles' sister. The vicar was so confused by this that he entered both brides as "Ann". It is unlikely that Tabitha could read at this stage of Verwood life, so she probably never knew of this mistake on her marriage certificate.

THE CRAFTS

THE BROOM MAKER

When Pam Reeks went to interview Alfie Sims, at his cottage off Lake Road, for a thesis in 1966, he was already then seventy-three years old. He told her of his family's involvement in the business and the difference between heather and birch based brooms.

His grandfather travelled by horse and wagon selling besoms from door to door from Verwood to Warminster and on to Andover. His turning point was Andover as besoms were made at Tadley and were sold between there and Andover. His father also made besoms which were taken by horse and wagon, together with pots from the Verwood pottery, westward across Dorset as far as Portland.

When Mr. Sims was working full time he often travelled into the New Forest to cut heather as did many other local broommakers. Then he cut it locally but was afraid that the Forestry Commission planting over Ringwood Forest would eventually kill all that supply. He chose a patch about three feet high, cut it with a reap hook and tied the heather into bundles, each containing enough for approximately six besoms. As heather can be cut all year round, he cut fifty to sixty bundles at a time and had them delivered to his workshop.

To make a heather besom, he untied a bundle and took out the pieces, longer ones first, and added them one by one until he had worked the required amount to his satisfaction. He then proceeded to make a round bunch from the smaller shoots, placing it on top of the first one. He then made another identical to the first so that the rounded bunch "the secret of a good foundation" lay between.

The bond which held the root or "butt" end of the heather used to be a six foot length of willow or hazel but in later years wire was used as in this case. It is pushed into the body of the besom then wound round and round and tightened by standing on the broomhead and pulling hard. The butt end was put on a chopping block to be neatened.

Mr. Sims then demonstrated the making of a birch broom and began by making a bond from a six foot length. With a knife, he removed all the knots to prevent cutting his hands on them as he worked and then twisted the twig from the top, peeling off the soft bark. Birch brooms are made all of a piece so he selected the correct lengths and worked them round in his lap to the correct sized head. He then sharpened the bond and threaded it into the butt, as for the heather besom, twisting it continually as he wound it round and round the head. Again it was tightened by standing on the head and pulling.

The handles were made from thicker branches of birch which he cut to length, trimmed to a point and neatened the ends. He then sat astride his "horse" to shave the wood which was held securely in a support, the blade being part of an old reap hook, bent by a blacksmith for the purpose.

The butt ends of the besom heads were then set to soak in boiling water in an old iron cauldron supported by bricks with a fire underneath.

The first bond was then tightened and a second bond made, both being pulled tight and trimmed. The pointed end of the handle was then hammered into the centre of the head with a wooden mallet. As the butt dries it tightens round the handle. The final stage is inserting the peg. A nail was hammered through the heather besom head into the handle and for the birch broom he similarly fixed a wooden peg into a pre-drilled hole.

Mr. Sims won many besom making awards at Agricultural Shows including the New Forest Show and the Bath and West Show. At that time he could sell as many besoms as he could make, supplying Racing Stables, Bournemouth and Weymouth Corporation Parks Departments and several private individuals who had used his services for many years. When he was working full time he could make twenty-four besoms a day. The only thing he could do by lamplight was to twist the bonds. He said that the heads could only be made in daylight or they would have looked more like birds' nests!

Tightening the bond on a birch broom

Boiling the heads in an iron kettle

Shaving the handle astride his "Broommaker's Horse"

MR. ALFIE SIMS OF LAKE ROAD IN 1966

Left: John Haskell senior was still an active broommaker up to the last decade of his life. He died in 1926 at the ripe old age of 90. Right: His son also John Haskell born 1876, seen here with Reg Hayward, followed his father's trade. Their workshop was in St. Stephen's Lane, Verwood. John jnr also acted as an amateur barber, cutting hair at night by the light of a candle held by his daughter Maud. She was warned not to hold it so close that wax dripped onto the customer's neck!

FRANK KEITH born 1883, son of Mark and Frances, was from one of the
Three Legged Cross group of broommaking families.

THE CRAFTS

THE HURDLE MAKER

Fred Kerley had been making hurdles in hazel coppices in and around Verwood for more years than anyone cares to remember, having followed his father into the trade. He cut in rotation around various locations for the landowners. In this way, an inexhaustible supply of material was maintained. In the early days of the Verwood Historical Society in the late 1970s or early 1980s, members spent a pleasant and informative evening with Fred being shown his craft and enjoying a running commentary. Fred appeared to be very content spending each and every day about the woodland, with only his radio for company. On this particular evening the gnats were biting ferociously but Fred was either impervious to them or very well protected. The members suffered in the pursuit of knowledge! The story of hurdle making continues as told to Pam Reeks. The complicated procedure described progresses smoothly in the hands of such an expert.

"Wood ten to twelve years old is the best as a lot of usable wood can be cut. Hazel bushes benefit from cutting as they throw up more shoots. It is softer and consequently easier to cut in the summer than in winter as frosts can make it brittle and difficult to work. If willow is used it has to be worked immediately after cutting as when it dries or is burned by the sun it becomes very brittle.

Fred Kerley – Hurdle Maker

The frame of the hurdle, a round log approximately seven feet long is pegged into the ground. Holes are drilled with an auger, into which the upright poles or "zales" are placed. The wood for the zales has to be fairly straight and is split to size with a cleaving hook. The hook point has to be sharp and the main blade blunt. Fred cut into the top with the sharp end and split the wood with the blunt part. The zale points were cut with a "knobby" knobbying hook which had a ten inch blade and had most of the weight at the head.

Smaller pieces had been put into bundles for "pea sticks". This wood was only eight years old but the owners had wanted it cut at the time rather than let it grow another few years. If Fred had not cut it then someone else would. Other by-products of hurdle making were the liggers and spars used by the thousand in the thatching trade.

Ten zales were put into the frame with any natural curve towards the front, away from him. He then chose smaller wood to continue the hurdle, picking up the pieces with the hook to prevent catching hold of thorns, or in the summer to prevent picking up snakes. Each piece had the knots or spikes trimmed off, this process being called "shredding". It was then split beginning approximately twelve inches from the top and splitting to the bottom. Mr. Kerley said that the rods to be woven can be used cloven or split if the rods are thick.

He began by weaving the four bottom binders or rods leaving the long ends free. Two "Johnny" rods (the name given to the next pair of rods) are woven, both being twisted round the end zale at the left. Bottom binders are twisted round the end zales next to form the "big spurs". These hold the bottom of the hurdle firm. Four or five "backers" (filling rods) are then woven, being twisted around the end zale on the right. The width of the hurdle is measured with a marked stick to ensure it is being made accurately.

Hurdles are six feet long. If the hurdle is to be for six foot high fencing, backers are used from the next rod up to the top binders. Sheep hurdles are three feet high of weaving plus the spike ends. If a sheep hurdle is being made, the pitch rod is the next rod woven. It is twisted round the left zale and threaded from the back to the front, four rods down. Next, a gap called a "twilly hole" is left in the weave of a sheep hurdle. Above this are woven two strong "twilly rods" which strengthen the hurdle for the occasions when the shepherd comes to move the fold.

Robert Morey and his father Edwin Thomas Morey (of Morey's Quarries) inspecting folded sheep. The "Twilly Hole" left for the Shepherd to move this type of hurdle is seen far right.

Two or three backers are then woven and twisted round the right hand zale. This end is then higher than the left because of the twisted rods. The top "binders" are then woven with the twists round the left end zale to help level the rods. To level the work completely, a short stiff rod called the "stumpy rod" is woven from the left end zale to the third zale from the right. The "pitch rod" is the final rod to be woven.

It is tucked in from the back, four rods down and twisted round the right end zale, the opposite way from the other rods, and woven through the top binders. The uneven ends are then trimmed. As Fred Kerley put it "trimming requires skill". One false cut could ruin the hurdle or injure the craftsman.

Hurdles have to be made with a slight curve but when they are stacked they straighten out. If they were straight, they would become curved when stacked. Completed fencing hurdles are not intended for portability once in place so there is no need for a twilly hole. Garden hurdles can be up to 6 feet high. When high hurdles are made the frame has to be placed in a trench or tilted and the hurdle made at an angle."

As their use in farming died out, the hurdles were taken up for domestic fencing and ornamental use. The wattle weave can also be adapted for use in rustic garden furniture. Well within living memory there used to be a constant stack of hurdles awaiting collection on a patch of grass on the corner of Station and Dewlands Roads, near to Thorne's Timber Mill in Verwood. Louis Lockyer only retired from full time hurdle making for Thorne's in May 1999 and eventually fully retired in 2001.

WOMEN'S WORK is proverbially never done. In the 19th and early 20th century a few had their own business such as dressmaking, millinery and laundry. For those with no stated profession their workload was none the less demanding in an age without any kind of labour saving gadget or even running household water. They practised their skills within the home environment. In olden times, many of the men wore elaborate smocks when about their daily work. In 1929 Lot Oxford recalled his grandparents' memories of Daniel Haskell (c.1790-1875 – father of John Haskell senior, broommaker). "He always wore a Smock Frock as nearly all the men in those days and they were wonderfully good things because they covered up all the other and I can well remember they used to make Pocket Handkerchiefs out of them". This intricate stitchcraft and the production of everyday clothes would have been the province of the womenfolk, trained to it from early childhood.

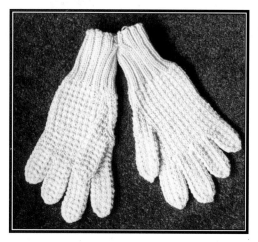

An example of Verwood Gloves knitted by Mrs. Helen Bailey to traditional pattern

Glove making was a cottage industry on the Hampshire-Dorset border at the beginning of this century. Several Verwood ladies could remember, as children, having to knit the ribbings of the gloves ready for their mothers to complete them. Boys as well as girls were taught these simpler parts. One lady said that knitting was always in her mother's hands, even as she walked about the house and garden. She could not remember the pattern as she was never entrusted to complete a glove. Others say that a Verwood woman's hands were never still and knitting was carried out leaning over the gate talking to neighbours.

Verwood gloves were highly prized in the area for their quality and hard wearing capability. They were made in men's, women's and children's sizes and often used for riding gloves. A representative of Cox and Hicks, the former Ringwood clothing and drapery retailer, used to bring the soft string with which they were made and collect the finished items on a regular basis. It is believed a man also used to come from Blandford once a fortnight for the same purpose. The money earned was a very welcome addition to the family budget. Incidentally in 1881 Jesse Davis from a Woolsbridge family, then aged 13, was apprenticed to Messrs. Charles Cox & Arthur Tom Hicks. He married Mr. Hicks' niece and took over the business which remained in family hands until its closure in 1989.

THE POTTERIES

Pottery was the major Verwood industry with its wares carried and known all over the surrounding area and even exported via Poole to Newfoundland and other countries. Clay was easily dug from the commons and brushwood for firing obtained free of charge from the same source. Numerous family enterprises sprang up all over the surrounding area extending south to Horton and north to Alderholt though Verwood retained its generic name. The stock in trade was utilitarian domestic earthenware, production methods remaining unchanged over the centuries. This lack of modernisation brought several interested visitors to the Crossroads Pottery to observe how similar domestic potteries would have operated in days before mechanisation and electricity. Amongst them were the famous St. Ives potter, Bernard Leach, and the antiquarian General Pitt-Rivers who commissioned the Verwood potters to make reproductions of his Mediterranean finds. A short, informative newsreel was filmed in 1917 and newspapers of the 1930s also ran several feature articles.

A Selection of Verwood Pottery including the evocative Costrel or "Cider Owl"

Prior to this the countryside around had been dotted with numerous other kilns, the major family producers being the Andrews of Margards Lane, Baileys of Ringwood Road and Springfield Road, Shearings of Dewlands Way, Hennings of Prairie Farm just over the Horton parish border and the Sims of Newtown Road, Black Hill and Springfield Road. Other potters known to operate in Verwood in the mid 1800s were James Bailey of Horton Way, James Budden and Charles King.

A kiln excavated at Ebblake by Verwood & District Potteries Trust in 1997 revealed a much older site dating back to the 1700s with ware of finer quality than that of the later manufacture. It is probable that when the clay and nearby firewood were exhausted the potters just moved on to another suitable location. They were frequently blamed in early documentation for not filling in the pits they had dug to the hazard of the population.

THE POTTERIES

CROSSROADS POTTERY

Robert Shearing was the first recorded tenant of the Crossroads Pottery in 1847, the land and premises then owned by "Squire" William Rolles Fryer. Robert's sister Louisa was married to the potter William Sims, it appears at the tender ages of 15 and 19, and through their nine children they became ancestors of many different Verwood family lines.

An omission from the above list are the names of Paul Ferrett and his sons who had no recorded pottery of their own but almost certainly worked alongside Robert Shearing whose wife Jane was Paul's sister. When Robert Shearing died in 1877 without a son, control of the Crossroads Pottery passed to the Ferrett side of the family. Paul Ferrett and his wife Hannah Read had had six sons and three daughters born at the cottage now known as "The Skep" in Dewlands Way. All of the sons worked at the pottery at some time but it was the youngest Charles or "Charlie" as he was generally known, who took over as Pottery Manager and later styled himself as Pottery Earthenware Manufacturer on the 1901 census. The third son, Amos, had opted for a different lifestyle as an Alehouse Keeper in London and was Publican of the "Duke of Wellington" in Bromley, Kent in 1901. One of Paul and Hannah's daughters, Ann, married Robert Sims of the Newtown Road pottery.

When Charlie Ferrett died in 1916 it was inherited by his eldest son, Fred Fry who used his mother Rose's maiden surname. Fred was a Master Potter of renown and an extremely talented musician who encouraged the youth of the village in this pursuit by forming a Methodist Boys' Band. Fred sold the Pottery, together with a large stock of ware, to Robert Thorne, Timber Merchant in 1925. Robert's son, Horace Thorne, continued to run the business under the management of Meshech Sims, the Master Potter, until his retirement in 1943. Meshech was the son of Seth who had been the potter at Black Hill and was himself the son of William Sims and Louisa Shearing.

The other working Master Potter, Herbert "Bert" Bailey continued the operation aided by Len Sims, until the pottery's closure in 1952. In 1901 there had been ten employees, in 1922 eight, by 1926 approximately five and by the 1940's only two remained.

As demand for heavy duty earthenware decreased, attempts were made to produce fancy goods such as posy bowls. Miniature cider "owls" or costrels were filled with lavender from Broadstone and sold by Liberty in London whilst miniature bricks were impregnated with the same scent or moth repellent to store amongst clothes. Between 1948 and 1950, Miss Gertrude Gilham, an experienced potter from Poole, also worked at the Crossroads Pottery. She used an electric wheel and kiln and produced tableware, much of which was sold in London. However these enterprises failed to stave off the inevitable fashion for less rustic goods and the pottery closed its doors in 1952.

The building was used as a tearoom and craft shop, by decorators Cox & Guy then Baileys' Electrical shop before being opened as a Hardware store "The Potter's Wheel" by Val Cutler whose husband Tony operated his plumbing business from the rear cob workshed. When Val retired in 1996 the building was donated to the town by the owners, Robert Thorne Ltd., and moves were put afoot to preserve it as an almost unique example of the former potters' working conditions. Building regulations decreed that the single skin brick lean-to at the front be demolished but this had the advantage of exposing the cob wall of the original shed. After several years of determined effort the restored building was opened in 2003 as Verwood Heathland Heritage Centre. This now forms a very attractive focal point, fronting onto Ferrett Green which, originally gravelled then hard surfaced, had served for many years as the town centre car park. Long before, this area had been the original mudpit for the pottery but when that supply was exhausted clay was brought initially from Holwell by horse and cart. The claypit was filled in in the late 19th century as being a danger to children.

Photographs on the following pages were all taken at the Crossroads Pottery in the earlier half of the twentieth century. They show the progression in the manufacturing process from raw clay to the finished product.

Above: Len Sims "wedges" or treads the wet clay to achieve an even consistency and to remove any stones and imperfections. The floor is strewn with sand to prevent sticking and Len supports himself with a pole. This scene took place in a brick lean-to attached to the cob workshed. After the pottery closed this area became "The Potters Wheel" Tearooms and then Hardware Store. It is now the outside patio of Verwood Heathland Heritage Centre.

Below: Master Potter, Meshech Sims, throws the clay in a corner of the workroom whilst Harold Churchill turns the wheel by means of a pole. Little verbal communication was needed between the Potter and his lad as experience dictated the speed of the wheel at various stages. The pencil-like stick projecting from the splashboard was used as a measure.

Above: In fine weather, work could take place out of doors in the large pottery yard. Here a party of visiting ladies admires the art. Master Potter, Bert Bailey, on the left demonstrates the making of jugs. His "lad" turns the wheel in a rotary fashion by means of a type of bicycle wheel attachment. On the right, Meshech Sims makes bushel pans, used for storing flour and other dry goods. Behind the land can be seen rising to the kiln mound.

Below: Several outbuildings stood around the yard, of cob and thatch or corrugated iron. Wood could be stacked for firing, handles fixed to jugs and pots laid out to dry in the open air. Above the cob workroom, a series of racks allowed the pots to be dried when the weather was inclement and these were heated from below by a fire or in later years a "tortoise" stove.

Above: At the rear of the cob workshop Bert Bailey and Meshech Sims supervise the laying out of the pots to dry. As well as bushel pans, a great many flower pots have been made for this firing. The pots would then be loaded into a huge brick lined earth mound with a flue at the bottom into a firing shed where brushwood kindling and later more substantial timber pieces were introduced. The kilns "burned" for two or three days, depending on the Master Potters' experience, sending plumes of smoke into the Verwood sky. As one little girl put it on a postcard to a sister away from home "Father is Burning". Another young lad used to curl up in the firing shed on cold winter nights as it was much warmer than sleeping at home.

Below: The pots were stacked from the bottom of the kiln to the top by means of ladders from the exit hole and placed according to their shape and type. The hole was then sealed and reopened a few days after the kiln had fired and cooled. Meshech Sims hands up the finished pots to Bert Bailey and their helpers. The glaze which had been applied before firing can be seen shining on the interior of the pot far right. Very few were glazed on the outside though jugs and costrels were thus finished below the rim and on the handles.

Left to Right: Jim Scammell, George "Drummer" Brewer, Len Sims, Meshech Sims, Bert Bailey

The men carry the finished ware down to the showroom and storage sheds. The height and structure of the kiln mound is clearly seen. The pots would then be sold locally or carried further afield by the higgler on his horse and cart. Many of the "Dealers in Brown Ware" as they were sometimes known were relatives of the various pottery owners helping to promote their own family enterprise. Others took it up as a self-employed trade.

Left to Right: Jim Scammell, Bert Bailey, Meshech Sims, Len Sims and Harold Churchill

The workforce is justly proud of its latest endeavours. On show are some of the more recent fancy goods as well as the age old staples. After decades "in the wilderness" lying forgotten in garden or shed, Verwood Pottery has now enjoyed a renaissance as a collector's item, admired for its rustic simplicity, satisfying shapes and warm ruddy or yellow colouration.

THE POTTERIES

"SANDALHOLME", MARGARDS LANE

Henry Andrews with his wife "Ketty" Shearing worked at this site in 1847 and probably from long before as they had married in 1814.   Keturah died in Verwood in 1855 but when Henry died in 1860 he was living at Thorn Hill in the New Forest.   Their son, Stephen, had married Jemima Bailey in 1851 and took over operations.   Stephen obviously felt he had to supplement his family's income as in December 1859 he was confined in Dorchester Gaol for a first offence of poaching (a common Verwood pastime).   From this we learn that he was 5ft 6¼ ins tall with dark brown hair, dark grey eyes and a sallow complexion.   At that time he was married with four children and his incarceration must have been a sore trial to the family.

Stephen's eldest son Job married Mary Davis in July 1876.   She had been born at Woolsbridge and was a sister of Mark and Samuel Davis of Holly Cottage, Manor Road.   Almost exactly two months after their wedding his father was dead aged only 48 but his widow, Jemima, continued living with Job and his family.   Job was still a Potter in 1901 but thereafter it appears he closed this kiln.   He only had two daughters, Peace and Charity, and so there were no sons to carry on the trade. He probably moved away from Verwood as there is no record of a burial for either him or Mary.   In 1901 both daughters were in service in Winchester to two separate clergymen of the city who were, however, brothers.

Stephen's younger son, Joseph, married Leah Naomi Haskell, former Pupil Teacher at the Church School, in 1879 and moved to another part of the village. He was however listed as a Potter's Labourer in 1881 and thereafter as a Hawker and so was likely to be taking his brother's goods away for sale.   Joseph and Naomi were the parents of Albert Andrews, the renowned Verwood craftsman and his sisters Beatrice and Winifred.

The house now named "Sandalholme" is one of the best preserved sites in Verwood with the kiln mound still intact and some of the outbuildings restored and incorporated into a beautiful house.

DEWLANDS WAY

Joseph Shearing, married to Rebecca White and a brother of Keturah Andrews, was the potter here until his death in 1846.   He was a first cousin, once removed, of Robert Shearing of the Crossroads Pottery.   His son Henry, married to Margaret Turner, owned the land and buildings in 1847 following his father in the trade.   In this year Rebecca, Joseph's widow, owned a piece of land and Chapel nearby on the common.   By April 1881, Henry, then a widower who died later that year, had retired, in favour of his son Joseph James known as James or "Jimmy" married to the aptly named Anna Potter. He continued the pottery at least until 1901, assisted by his son Henry, and died in 1913.   Another son William "Willie" opted for a life on the railways eventually becoming an Engine Driver for LSWR.

The single storey pottery house on this site was demolished about 2001 and the land cleared for new housing. The kiln mound had not survived.

JOSEPH & FRANK SHEARING

These two unmarried brothers, born 1843 and 1854, were almost consistently listed as Potters throughout the later 19th century including the 1901 census, although in 1891 their occupation was that of Labourers.   They were first cousins of James Shearing of Dewlands Way and second cousins of Job Andrews of Margards Lane and lived somewhere around the same area. It may be that they operated an independent kiln as yet unidentified or that they assisted one or other of their cousins.   There were other relatives of the large Shearing contingent who worked at various potteries throughout the nineteenth century.

THE POTTERIES

"MOOR LODGE", RINGWOOD ROAD AND SPRINGFIELD ROAD (1)

James Bailey married Ann Shearing, sister of Ketty and Joseph, who died in 1849. James was the Potter at the Ringwood Road site in 1847 though on the Tithe Apportionment and Map he is shown as occupying two properties owned by William Bailey, most probably his younger son, also a Potter and married with a young family. On the 1851 census James had only his unmarried daughter Leah living with him and it is possible they had moved to a cottage on the site or that William had built his own larger property.

James' elder son Thomas Bailey had married Jane Mesher in 1838 and it appears had moved to the Springfield Road site where a Potter of that name was shown on the Tithe Schedule. At this time the site also contained a chapel which was probably the one fronting Manor Road, remembered until the early twentieth century as of Baptist denomination but long since demolished. On the 1851 census, although no specific address is given, Thomas appears to be living in this general area. The couple had six small children, though one, Enoch, died in 1852 and was buried in Verwood Churchyard.

Almost unbelievably, on 31st March 1853 both James and Thomas died, James aged 61 of Bronchitis lasting 5 days and Thomas aged 39 of Pneumonia which had lasted a week. One can only speculate what they had been doing the previous week and what weather they had been exposed to. They were both buried in Verwood Churchyard on 3rd April. This traumatic event robbed the family of two breadwinners at one stroke. Springfield Road may have been abandoned, at least in the short term.

Thomas' children were at the time far too young to take over the Springfield Road site and his widow and children did not live in Verwood thereafter. However, Thomas has a headstone in Verwood Churchyard and Jane is buried with him. When she died, she was living in Christchurch so it appears that she moved right away from this area. Less than two months after her father's death, Leah Bailey married George Ingram a long time widower whose sister had been married to Leah's first cousin, Henry Andrews, son of Henry & Keturah of the Margards Lane Pottery.

James' younger son, William continued at the Ringwood Road site. He was married to Emma Prince of Witchampton and all their four sons were at one time or another engaged in allied trades either as potters, brickmakers or ware hawkers. Their daughter Love was married in 1862 to Samuel Bailey who was most likely a cousin of her father although they were close in age. Samuel and Love were given as the main householders on the 1891 census with William, then aged 74, and Emma living with them in retirement.

Samuel was then the resident Potter, assisted by sons Albert and Eder with brother-in-law Ain Bailey as Potter's Labourer. Another brother-in-law, William Bailey married to his first cousin Augusta Ingram, was a Ware Dealer, on the road at "The Greyhound" Inn, Dorchester on that census, no doubt helping to distribute the family products.

In 1901 Samuel remained as Potter together with his eldest son Albert, his younger two sons, Eder and Fred, having gone into the bakery trade. Ain had died by then but William was still a Hawker. Sadly Albert died in 1911 at the age of 40, predeceasing his father by five years and his mother by ten. Samuel was aged 77 when he died in 1916 and it is presumed that work stopped either then or when Albert died though descendants of the family continued to live on at the house with the kiln and outbuildings abandoned.

The kiln and outbuildings at Moor Lodge survived unused until 1985 when, after an archaeological investigation, the site was cleared for a housing development which is now called Shard Close. It would be surprising indeed if pottery shards did not turn up from time to time in the gardens.

It is likely that Herbert John "Bert" Bailey, last Master Potter at the Crossroads, was Samuel's great-nephew and that his father was a second cousin of Love.

THE POTTERIES

BLACK HILL

Seth Sims, born 1847, developed this site. He was married in 1866 to his first cousin Sarah Sims, daughter of his uncle Joseph. His parents were William Sims and Louisa Shearing, who lived at the house later known as Pear Tree Cottage in Ringwood Road. William had had an interesting career, according to the census. In 1851 he was a Dealer in Brown Ware and in 1861 a Broom Maker. By 1871 he had become a Master Potter employing 5 men and 1 boy. However, in 1881 at the age of 74 he was described as a Labourer with the qualifying remarks "Journeyman Turf Cutter" added.

In 1871 and 1881 Seth was a Potter's Labourer working first for his father and then most probably for his brother Robert who had started a pottery in Newtown Road. Seth was a Potter in his own right by 1891 presumably having found a site just uphill from his brother. His youngest son, Meshech, who later became Master Potter at the Crossroads, was assisting him as his labourer whilst his son John and his married son Seth junior who lived next door were Ware Hawkers taking the goods for sale around and out of the village.

In 1901 Seth senior was still a Potter as was his son Seth who lived close by. John, now married, living in the same area, and Meshech still at home were Potter's Labourers.

Seth was a lifelong member of the Congregational Church, joining when it was still a mudwall Independent chapel on Church Hill. At his death in 1926 at the age of 79, he was the oldest member of the church. He was a Deacon, Sunday School Superintendent and a Trustee of the Silver Star Rechabite Tent of Verwood. This latter was a strictly teetotal organisation of which Seth was a staunch member. His funeral was conducted in Verwood Churchyard according to their rites.

Meshech, John, Seth jnr and Elizabeth – Children of Seth and Sarah Sims of Black Hill

The house still stands but the kiln mound was demolished at a later date to improve the appearance of the garden. Little did anyone think in those days that these disused appendages of a country pottery would have become fascinating relics of a bygone age.

THE POTTERIES

NEWTOWN ROAD OR LOWER BLACK HILL

Robert (William Robert) Sims, born 1838, Seth's older brother, established this pottery at the foot of Black Hill by 1881 having previously worked as an Agricultural Labourer. He was married to Ann Ferrett, daughter of the potter Paul Ferrett, his uncle Robert Shearing's business partner, in 1861. They lived at what is now known as "The Old Farmhouse" where according to descendants "Ann was most clean and particular and whitewashed the cottage inside and out once a year". This was the cottage lived in during the 1970s by Jessie Matthews, the musical comedy actress and now one of the most attractive buildings in Verwood. The pottery yard has been transformed into a large and beautiful garden.

Robert and Ann Sims' cottage in Newtown Road, which has since been extensively altered and extended.
At one time the single storey building on the right housed a Doctor's Surgery.

Robert styled himself a Farmer in 1901 and by that time or before he died in 1911 the pottery had closed. Only one of their six sons followed him into the pottery trade. One of their four surviving daughters, Kitty, married Sidney Palmer of the Ebblake Brickyard in 1907.

SPRINGFIELD ROAD (2)

Fred Sims, son of Robert and Ann of Newtown Road, was born in 1867 and married Anna Loader in 1892. Just before his marriage he was working as a Potter alongside his father but then took over the Springfield Road site, his first few children being born in the thatched cottage there. Fred became increasingly interested in building rather than pottery and the family lived in one of his new houses, "Maybank", in Manor Road, opposite what is now the "Monmouth Ash" public house before moving to Eastworth Farm as a tenant of Lord Normanton in 1915. He renovated the farmhouse and bought it from the Somerley Estate in 1919 together with surrounding farmland. Fred was responsible for several of the distinctive detached houses along Manor and Station Roads. The Springfield Road site has long been cleared and developed.

THE POTTERIES

PRAIRIE FARM, HORTON PARISH

A short way off Dewlands Road to the south of Does Lane lay the pottery site formerly known by this name. Although only just over the boundary, the building is in Horton Parish though would be considered part of Verwood for the everyday life of its inhabitants. Horton, for some unknown historical reason, takes a "wedge shaped bite" out of Verwood at this point, deviating from the River Crane. Donald Young's paper on the district's potteries, written in 1974, tells us that

> "Prairie Farm probably ceased work about 1840. The Horton Tithe Map of 1841 shows it as house and buildings not a pottery. Occupier Richard Henning aged 69. He is listed as a potter in the 1821 Census Returns [when basic occupational information was collected] but a yeoman in his will of 1843. He was a man of substance, leasing a considerable amount of land and several cottages in Verwood which he left to his four sons at his death. Pottery was probably only one of his interests and was not carried on by any of his sons although the youngest, John, occupied the property until at least the 1860s.
>
> Richard's son Job spent a month in Dorchester Gaol in 1839 for trespassing and poaching and was then described as a potter whilst in his father's will he is a labourer. It is likely, therefore, that the kiln ceased between 1839 and 1841. A large oak tree on the kiln mound which obviously grew after the kiln became disused confirms this date."

The house has been restored and several outbuildings remain. Several members of the extended Henning family found their marriage partners in Verwood and so became ancestors of later generations on this side of the parish boundary.

HORTON WAY

The 1900 revision of the Ordnance Survey map shows a large plot on the north-west corner of Horton Way and Margards Lane marked as a pottery. This was also technically part of Horton, the parish boundary running down the centre of Horton Way for a short distance before breaking off south to rejoin the River Crane. Again, this would have made little difference to the man or woman on the ground as it was an area quite divorced from the village of Horton itself. It would, however, have meant the inconvenience of travelling much further to their mother church for baptisms, marriages and burials although they lived just across the road from those with the parochial right of these ceremonies closer at hand.

This site belonged to yet another sprig of the Shearing family tree. Henry Shearing, who died in 1840, was a brother of Joseph, Keturah and Ann already mentioned. By 1851 his son William, married to Catherine Fry, was the Potter here. However he died in May 1858 aged 39 leaving Catherine with four small children. This date appears to coincide with the temporary appearance of two more Potters who may well have been relations helping out if not independent workers in their own right. Their credentials are given below.

William's brother John had already died having married Mary Ann Bailey who by then had remarried to Charles Harvey. Their brother Joseph had become a Blacksmith on a nearby piece of land, thereafter known as Forge Lane, founding a dynasty spanning several generations. Therefore there was no immediate family to carry on the business.

Of William and Catherine's children, George became a Ware Hawker, marrying Ann Budden, daughter of James and Mary Ann below, whilst Mary Elizabeth married her second cousin Jeremiah Shearing, another Potter, who died young. In 1871 Catherine, as Kitty, is living with the widowed Mary Elizabeth and her daughter Maria in Horton parish, perhaps in the same house but not described as a pottery. It appears that this kiln had been abandoned as no further mention of it is made in official records.

Whilst the Shearing surname has many variations such as Shering and Sherring, it has here been standardized to that more usually adopted by the Verwood branches.

THE POTTERIES

JAMES BUDDEN

James Budden most likely lived on the north side of Does Lane off Dewlands Road with land on the south side in Horton parish adjoining Prairie Farm. He may have been a relation of William Shearing of Horton Way pottery whose grandmother had been Joanna Budden. He had been born around 1811 in Woodlands and was married to Mary Henning at Horton with Woodlands on 23rd October 1835. Mary is named in some records as Mary Ann and was most likely the daughter of Richard and Elizabeth Henning baptised 4th May 1817 at Horton and sister of Job of Prairie Farm.

James was a Labourer but first appears as a Potter at the baptism of their daughter Jane in 1858 and again on the 1861 census when his son Charles is also given that trade. At the time of the census on the night of 2nd/3rd April 1871 James was on his deathbed with his wife, six surviving unmarried children and two married children in the house with another married son William next door. Also at home was their lodger, George Guy, who was to marry their daughter Emily. James was buried a week later on 10th April. Their eldest son, Frederick, was the Police Constable of the village of Charles in Devon and a daughter Ann was married locally to George Shearing, as has been seen. Both of these have the distinction of being recorded on the census not only at their parents' house but also at their normal dwelling places.

In 1871 James was again given as an Agricultural Labourer but his son Frank was a Potter's Labourer. Also their son William and his lodger, a widower named James Bailey, were Potter's Labourers. Mary Ann was given of no profession but on the 1881 census is herself a Potter with her son Frank as a General Labourer. It may be that Mary Ann inherited her talent from her Henning forebears but hid her light under a bushel whilst her husband was alive.

Roland Budden, Coal Merchant. Son of Lot and grandson of James and Mary Ann

None of their children followed in the trade. Frederick continued his career in Devon whilst the youngest, Lot, became a Coal Merchant and Dealer. The other sons worked as Labourers. Their son William married Eliza Jean Henning, daughter of Thomas, in 1866 who was very likely his cousin. It seems therefore that there was a dual connection between the Henning and Budden families who lived so close to each other albeit in different parishes.

THE POTTERIES

JAMES BAILEY

James Bailey, born 1826, was the youngest of six children of William Bailey, Carpenter and his wife Elizabeth who lived in what is now known as Forge Lane, Verwood. His sister Mary Ann had married John Shearing of the Horton Way pottery family and they were also near neighbours of Henry Andrews of the Margards Lane pottery. James was married in 1849 at Lyndhurst in the New Forest to Portsmouth born Jane Hatch. The couple made their home on a smallholding at Cherry Tree Cottage, Horton Way in Verwood where all their thirteen children were born and then baptised at Verwood Anglican Church.

James spent most of his career as a Ware Hawker, perhaps collecting his goods from the nearby Shearing and Andrews' pottery as well as other outlets. He did though have a brief spell as a Potter himself around 1861 when he gave that profession on the census and also at the baptism of two of his children in 1859 and 1863 and again at the baptism of twins in 1874. At that of the children born in between he reverted to being a Hawker of Pottery. It seems, therefore, that his actual involvement in pottery making was minimal compared to the amount of time he spent selling it. It cannot have been an easy life for Jane with a smallholding and large family to cope with whilst her husband was out on the road. However, she must have thrived on it as she lived to the age of 85, dying in 1916 eleven years after her husband who had then been aged 73.

CHARLES KING

This Potter is something of an enigma, appearing to have come from nowhere to live in Verwood when he married Mary Ann Shearing, neé Bailey on 11th March 1848 at Cranborne Church. At that time he used the surname Harvey and gave no details of his father and on various census returns gave his birthplace as Christchurch Hants, Longham Dorset and Cranborne. Mary Ann was the older sister of James Bailey of Horton Way and had previously been married to John Shearing of the Horton Way pottery. She had three daughters when John died in 1847 and was living with her second husband, daughters and a new baby Job Harvey in 1851. Charles was at that time a Dealer in Brown Ware.

Charles and Mary Ann had another son, Charles, who died as an infant but on 23rd October 1858 they had a daughter Rose who was officially registered by her mother on 24th November as Rose Harvey, daughter of Charles – Potter (Master) and Mary Ann, late Shering, formerly Bailey. However she was baptised on 12th December 1858 at Verwood Independent Chapel as Rose King. From then on the family used this surname, Job Harvey also becoming Job King. This change of surname coincided with Charles becoming a Potter in his own right, employing 4 Labourers in 1861 and 2 men and 2 boys in 1871. By 1881, still a Potter, he was a widower with his stepdaughter Barbara Shearing as his housekeeper.

It is not easy to tell at which pottery Charles was operating though from his employment of others he clearly had his own site. From his approximate whereabouts in various census returns it is highly possible that he had resuscitated the Springfield Road site left vacant by Thomas Bailey in 1853 and before it was taken over by Fred Sims in 1892.

The above is a brief resumé of the lives of Verwood's major potters. There were a few others such as James Shearing, another nephew of Joseph, Henry, Keturah and Ann, born 1806 at Eastworth, who married Ann, daughter of Independent Minister Jeremiah Argyle. James was operating in 1851 and 1861, though exactly where is not known. In addition there were small enterprises combined with other occupations such as Charles Butler, Farmer at Burrows Farm, where it is known a kiln mound existed, who also called himself a Potter in 1861.

Much interesting and informative material about the early history of the Verwood and District Potteries with technical details of its manufacture has been written elsewhere and so is not covered in the scope of this book.

THE POTTERIES

GENEALOGY OF THE VERWOOD POTTERS AND THEIR KILNS

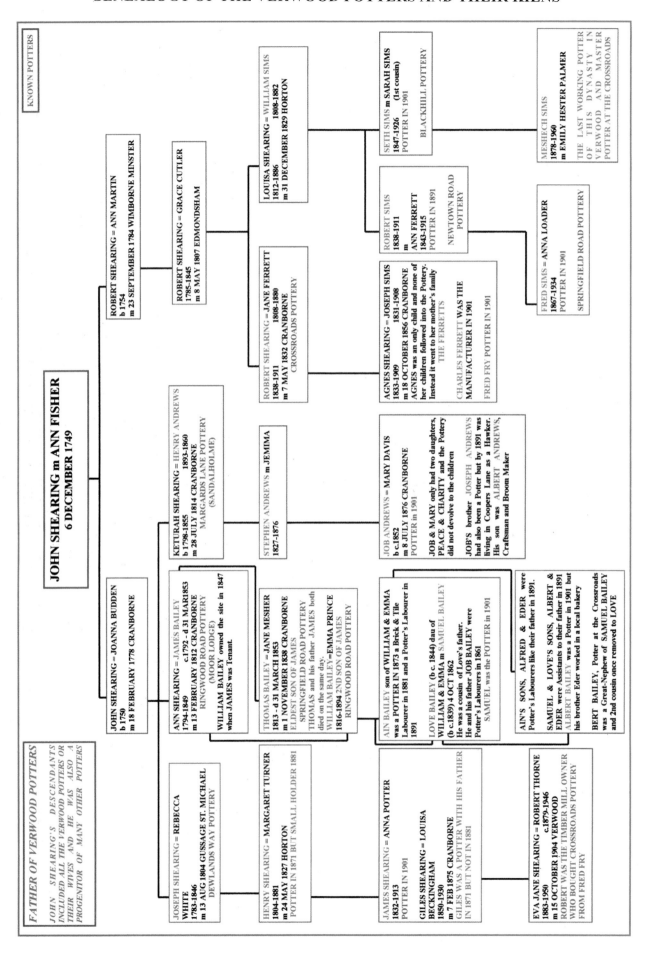

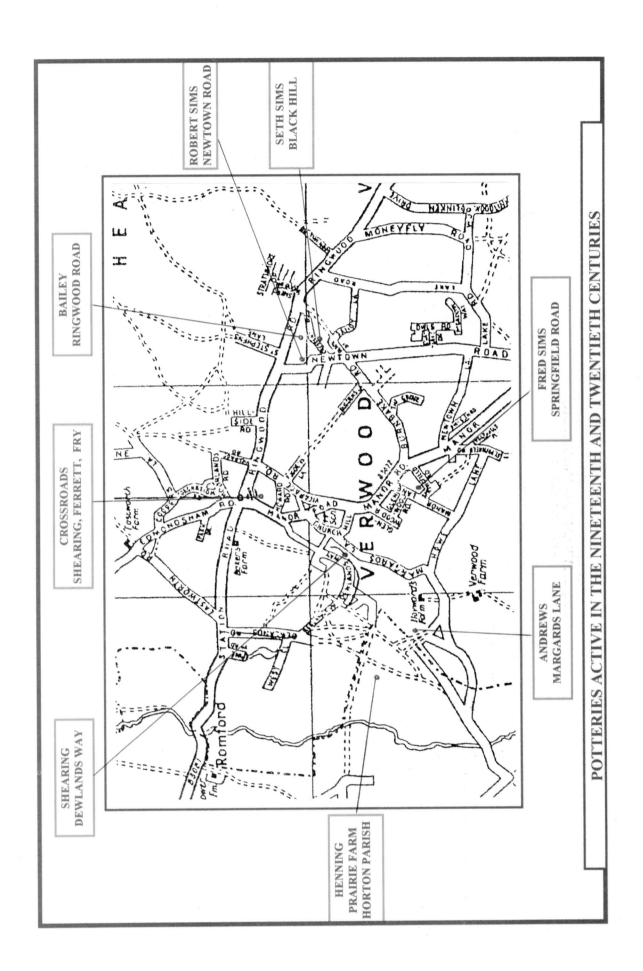

ROBERT SIMS
NEWTOWN ROAD

SETH SIMS
BLACK HILL

BAILEY
RINGWOOD ROAD

FRED SIMS
SPRINGFIELD ROAD

CROSSROADS
SHEARING, FERRETT, FRY

SHEARING
DEWLANDS WAY

ANDREWS
MARGARDS LANE

HENNING
PRAIRIE FARM
HORTON PARISH

POTTERIES ACTIVE IN THE NINETEENTH AND TWENTIETH CENTURIES

THE BRICKWORKS

Brickmaking was another major Verwood industry founded on the underlying clay soil. Local estates such as Somerley owned by Lord Normanton and Wimborne St. Giles owned by Lord Shaftesbury had their own brickyards for the construction of their farmhouses and outbuildings but self-built, "cob" mudwall cottages were the normal dwellings of ordinary villagers at least up to the latter part of the nineteenth century and in several cases beyond.

The first consistent Verwood brickmakers were Joseph Andrews (1797-1851) and his three sons. Joseph senior, previously an Agricultural Labourer, died in December 1851. Two of his sons left the village but Joseph junior (1827-1896) continued in this trade until in 1881, by then living in Ringwood Road, he rose to be the Foreman of a Brickworks.

Commercial brickmaking began in Verwood in the late nineteenth and early twentieth centuries. At its height there were four yards in operation, the Manor Works on Black Hill owned by Squire Fryer and family, the Verwood & Gotham Brick and Tile Company yard behind the Station, Hopkins' yard in the same area but set back on the northern side of the Cranborne Road and the Ebblake yard, just over the county boundary in Hampshire.

Working in the Brickfields at Boys Wood, Sutton near Verwood

By 1881 an organized brickyard, of which Joseph Andrews was the foreman, had obviously been started somewhere in Verwood and by the location of its foreman and workers' houses around Ringwood Road and Newtown, it is probable that it was the beginning of the Manor Brickworks on Black Hill. On the 1900 OS map a hatched line containing two shed shaped buildings is shown on this site. Two brickyards were marked as such, that at the Station and another behind Somerly Cottage on the road to Cranborne. The latter was probably an estate brickyard, not worked in living memory, the land being owned in the early 19th century by Lord Shaftesbury and later by Lord Normanton.

Just before 1891 Arthur Hopkins, born in Holt but recently of Kinson, came with his family to live in Ringwood Road, giving his occupation as a Brickmaker. Married to Verwood born Sarah Brewer, there also appears to have been a close family connection with Joseph Andrews and it is likely he began work at the Manor Yard. About the same time Arthur's brother Henry Charles and family moved into the village from Bere Regis. Charles, also a Brickmaker, lived in the Dewlands Common area and may have been working at the brickyard then in operation by the Station. By 1901 Arthur had risen to become a Brick Manufacturer and had moved house to Vicarage Road. Job Brewer, his wife's first cousin, later also a builder and Justice of the Peace, gave the same occupation and from documents dated a few years after was Lessee and Manager of the Manor Brickworks. Job is listed in 1911 Kelly's directory as a brickmaker but his younger brother Harry Brewer and his sons shortly took over the Manor Yard where they remained for many years until its closure.

THE BRICKWORKS

From Christmas Day 1906 Arthur Hopkins, trading as A & S. Hopkins, leased land north of the Station from Lord Normanton for a period of 21 years which became a Brick and Tile Yard. Presumably this was in conjunction with his son Sidney, then aged 26, his eldest son Frederick Jesse having become a Primitive Methodist Minister. The property was a surface rental with royalties to be paid on bricks manufactured from the underlying earth. Arthur Hopkins bought the yard from the Somerley Estate in 1919 though later it came under the ownership of the Verwood & Gotham Brick and Tile Company who already owned the Station Brickworks. Arthur also signed a 99 lease for his nearby house on 25th March 1907 at a Ground Rent of £1 per annum. This was built of brick at a cost of £300 and had four bedrooms and two sitting rooms with the other usual offices. In the mid 1920s he bought the newsagency at the Crossroads for his unmarried daughter Nellie and having by then lost his wife and three sons, two including Sidney in the First World War, it is believed he spent his declining years with her there.

Somerley Brickworks at Ebblake

A disused Somerley Estate Brickworks site at Ebblake had been revived before 1891 by William Palmer, an experienced brickmaker, and family from Wyke Regis, West Dorset. This yard made the famous white bricks which formed decorative patterns on many buildings all over the surrounding area. William was assisted by some of his sons but the yard closed in the early twentieth century when the clay ran out.

It appears that the Station Brickworks was redeveloped in 1913 by the Verwood & Gotham Brick and Tile Company as their lease, also owned by Lord Normanton, ran from then for 40 years. This presumably was when the kilns, chimneys and associated buildings were erected. William Palmer's son Sidney later became its Manager and Salesman, cycling within a 20 mile radius for orders. He remained there until just before WWII when it was taken over by the Southern United Brick Company.

Squire Henry Charles Fryer was not slow in following suit. A warrant granted by the Royal Courts of Justice under the Settled Land Acts in April 1914 gave him permission, under a Family Trust, to carry out his intended modernisation of the Manor Yard. Works estimated at a total of £1,750 included a modern kiln with twelve chambers, flues and a shaft to carry off the smoke, a drying shed, crushing and pressing machines with an engine to drive them, an engine house and a cottage for the foreman or engine driver who would also act as caretaker. The cottage was to contain an office for the Lessee's use, by this time confirmed as Job Brewer, who had sworn an affidavit in support.

The former Hopkins' Tileyard had closed in the early 1930s and the Station Brickworks at the start of the Second World War. Both were then owned by the Southern United Brick Company who went into voluntary liquidation and sold them at auction in 1947.

Building the kilns and chimney at Fryer's Manor Brickworks

Bricks from the village had a good reputation, enjoying a thriving home and export trade. Some special orders carried a "frog" indentation on the top with the name of the village or manufacturer though most were left plain.

Bournemouth Pavilion and the former Continental Cinema in Winton were built from Verwood brick whilst Blandford Army Camp was another major customer. Until 1910 bricks and tiles were taken to the surrounding villages and towns by horse and cart, the number of bricks per load depending on the size and ability of the horse. Some horses could pull as many as three hundred and fifty to four hundred bricks. After 1910 bricks from the Manor Yard were transported by Foden's steam lorries and could be taken greater distances. They were also sent further afield by rail where the Station Brickworks had sidings onto the line.

Working in the brickyards was an arduous task as Pam Reeks found out when she interviewed two former employees in 1966, Mr. E. Batten of the Manor Brickworks, also known as Blackhill, and Mr. Waters who had worked at the Tileyard. She later had many conversations with another employee of the Manor Brickworks, Mr. Arthur Spencer.

At the Manor Brickworks, the main part of their working day necessitated the clay being dug from the pits and mixed with loam or sand in an enormous pug mill. The clay was then forced into a long slab which was cut with cheese wires to the required size, producing ten bricks at a time. Before this mechanization, bricks had been hand made in moulds or in a presser which turned out one brick at a time. The wet blocks were then pulled onto a board and from there three boards of sixty bricks were placed on a brick-barrow. Each brick weighed ten pounds when wet and seven to eight pounds when dry so shifting them around the yard was strenuous work. When the weather was wet, the barrow took a great deal of strength to move. The bricks were then moved outside to dry in rudimentary wooden frames with a wooden or corrugated iron cap to keep out the rain. When dry, they were fired in a German type kiln with twelve chambers and three firing holes, used in rotation, so keeping them continuously in production.

The Manor Brickworks was always strongly associated with Verwood Band with preferential employment being given to those who could play an instrument. Men came from far and wide to work there for the twin benefits of employment and inclusion in the musical activities. Arthur Spencer's father, Tom, had been the Bandmaster in his day and Arthur also became a keen member although children in the 1970s might remember him better as their genial school bus driver. The Bandsmen were not, however, allowed time off work for their performances but had to make up their shift often in the very early morning so as to be ready to leave in time to travel to their engagement.

Again in the early 20th century Mr. Waters with his father and brothers, experienced tile makers from Sussex, had come to the Verwood and Gotham Brick and Tile Company's yard on the north-western fringe of the village to boost the output of tiles. Yellow and brown clay was dug at the site which together produced a good red colouring. Like Verwood bricks these earthen roofing tiles were in great demand both in the immediate area and far beyond.

THE BRICKWORKS

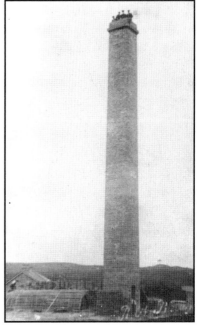

THE BEGINNING

Above: Building the Manor Brickworks chimney atop Black Hill in the early 20th century. All around is open heathland, long before the Forestry Commission planting. The pool at Higher Moor can clearly be seen as a lighter horizontal mark just to the left of the chimney.

Above right: The "topping out" ceremony on the completed chimney. One of the men is waving a flag. They most probably also took a camera or an intrepid photographer went aloft with them as a "Birds Eye View of Verwood" postcard looking up Ringwood Road must have been taken from this vantage point.

THE END

The deserted and overgrown Verwood & Gotham Brick and Tile Co. yard north of the Station. The yard closed about 1934 and lay derelict thereafter. In the 1950s it was bought by the Sims family of Eastworth Farm and the buildings used for storing hay etc. This was the last of the brickwork chimneys to be demolished and was a Verwood landmark for many years afterwards, its top visible above the surrounding tree cover. It was eventually taken down for safety reasons in October 1999.

THE BRICKWORKS

Again the clay, mixed with sand and water, was fed into a pug mill. The pug for tiles was much softer than that for bricks and was taken out in large chunks to be formed by hand. Mr. Waters said he "had to have a system" for making the tiles rapidly without wasted time and effort. A lump of clay was thrown into a sanded iron or wooden mould on the work bench, the top being levelled with wire and smoothed off with a wooden striker dipped in water. It was then set aside on the sanded floor. The tiles were then dried on racks until "leather hard" when they were beveled on a "wooden horse" and stacked in piles on the drying shed floor. When bone dry they were fired in Belgian type kilns along with bricks produced on the site. These had firing holes at intervals all round with one entrance for stacking and removing the bricks and tiles. Before 1924 twelve foot high, square Scotch kilns had been used which had no roof, the topmost layer of bricks being used to keep the heat in and to watched during firing to ascertain the amount of heat.

Workers outside a kiln at Verwood & Gotham Brick and Tile Company Yard

Back Row: 1. ? Waters 2. Arthur Groves 3. George Brewer 4. Billy Mills 5. Cecil Waters 6. Jack Shearing 7. Walt Potter
Front Row: 1. Len Read 2. Eder Bailey 3. ? Keevil 4. Arthur Bailey (Cripplestyle) 5. Victor Waters 6. Jack Read

The bricks were stacked at the bottom and around the sides of the kiln with the tiles in between. They were stacked on their bottom edge so that the lip at the top kept them separated, allowing the heat to travel between. The firing with coal took two days and nights, the fires being checked every two hours. The kiln was bricked up during firing but one brick left loose so that specimen tiles could be hooked out for testing. Once the firing was complete the kiln was left to cool.

Tiles were made in a variety of different shapes apart from the standard roofing tile, sizes including one and a half, half or slips, eave, ridge, hip and valley as well as decorative wall tiles. If the tiles were to be coloured differently from the usual red then the ingredients were mixed with sand and added at the moulding stage. Manganese and sand produced black tiles whilst manganese alone gave a purple tint. A mottled effect was obtained by sprinkling manganese over the tiles after they had been sanded. When green tiles were required, the tile makers had to tour the nearby fields collecting fresh cow manure. This was made into a solution with water and manganese and painted onto the surface.

Mr. Waters made an average of four thousand tiles per week for which he was paid thirty-two shillings but this included Sunday mornings at no extra pay. He and his family made tiles in Verwood for fifty years until the outbreak of World War II.

A kiln stacked at the Station Brickworks

Verwood's flourishing brick industry did not survive World War II. In some cases because the clay at a particular site had run out but the death knell was sounded when men were called up to the war and blackout regulations precluded the continuous firing process by which the kilns operated. Although there was talk of revival after the war, nothing came of it and so an important Verwood industry died.

THE VERWOOD & GOTHAM BRICK AND TILE WORKS AT ROMFORD
Artist's Reconstruction by Clive Daniels

THE SANDPITS

The quarry on the side of Stephen's Castle has always been referred to as "The Sandpits". It is an outcrop of pure sandstone of such good quality that it was in high demand not only locally in the brick, pottery and building businesses but exported by train to the glass and brick making industries, especially in South Wales. The presence of such sand in close proximity to major seams of clay had increased the ability of Verwood to become an industrial centre in the midst of an agricultural environment.

Verwood Sandpits

This was part of Boveridge Heath which had belonged to the Normanton estate at Somerley until 1919 when 7,650 acres around the surrounding area were auctioned off, the same sale in which Fred Sims bought Eastworth Farm. This particular lot of 672 acres included "A Bed of Clean Sharp Sand". Together with surrounding heathland it was bought by Mr. Sidney William Palmer, youngest son of William Palmer of Ebblake Brickyard. Sidney was married to Kitty Sims, daughter of Robert and Ann Sims of the Newtown Road pottery. His twin sister, Emily Hester Palmer, was married to Kitty's cousin Meshech Sims of the Black Hill and Crossroads potteries. As well as operating the sandpits, Mr. Palmer ran piped water from a nearby reservoir to residents on that side of the village.

Sadly, there was one fatality in 1935 when quarry worker, Harry Riggs, was buried alive in a sandslip after heavy rain. Frantic efforts to reach and rescue him tragically failed and he is buried in Verwood churchyard.

Sand ceased to be extracted in the early 1960s and thereafter the area lay disused with a band of gypsies camped there around 1967-68.

The enterprise finally closed in 1976-77 and is now a Nature Reserve under East Dorset Countryside Management.   It is a pleasant place for a stroll with magnificent views of the surrounding countryside and coast afforded from the top of Stephen's Castle which stands at 261 feet or just under 80 metres above sea level.

Verwood Sandpits.
Hand loading by horse and cart. The sand was taken to a site near the present Band Hall and collected from there by steam lorries which could not negotiate the narrow, bumpy lane to the quarry.

Gravel from Morey's quarries just to the east, now Tarmac, was also used in the construction of the Mulberry Harbours for the D Day invasion.   The Wimborne & District News of 27th May 1950, a special edition covering Verwood, tells us that also "In the weeks before the allied invasion sacks of the gravel were dropped into occupied France to be used by the Secret Service and French Maquis in the "hush-hush" construction of gun sites and runways. This is only part of the quarries' fascinating war-time history, for the majority of the pits were requisitioned by the Army and the first experimental Bailey bridges were thrown across the quarry lakes.

Over 30 men are employed by Moreys, quarry owners and haulage contractors, and the firm are proud of the fact that they are pioneers in the industry. Some of the men have been with the firm since its inauguration and the opening of the first quarries 30 years ago.

Methods of quarrying have altered considerably since the opening of the first gravel pit on the Somerley Estate, when picks and shovels were used and the gravel was screened by hand sieves or riddles. The men worked in pairs, with as many as 40 men in one pit. At that time most of the material was sold for road making and was used extensively in Dorset, Hants and Wiltshire. As there was found to be an accumulation of oversized material in the pits, a crushing process was started and this provided excellent material for concrete.

It was thanks to this stage in its development that the firm secured the contract to supply the material for the building of the Bournemouth Pavilion and, at a later date, the swimming baths also". Presumably these were the main Pier Approach baths which used to host Aqua Displays as well as public swimming but were demolished in the 1980s.

THE TIMBER MILLS

James Thorne came to live at Romford Mill, just inside Edmondsham parish in the late 1870s and on the 1881 census described himself as a Farmer and Miller. He started by collecting wheat from miles around, grinding it and returning the flour. In a small way he was also engaged in hurdle making, timber felling and saw milling and in 1891 was described as a Timber Merchant and Farmer.

Romford Mill and House with the Millstream

Towards the end of the century he also became an Agricultural Contractor, starting his own threshing business. The first machines were horse-drawn and powered, the team driving a windlass-like affair to provide motivation for the thresher. His son Robert took over shortly before his father died in 1910 by which time the threshing tackle and machines were drawn and powered by steam engines. In those days a man had to walk in front with a red flag of which Mr. Rose of Verwood was one. The engines had names such as "King of the Forest" and "Greyhound" and were always guaranteed to attract interest wherever they went.

In 1914 Robert purchased a new steam engine "The Romford Express" and its reception upon arrival in the village after a two-day journey from Basingstoke was almost as great as that given to the carnival procession of 1950 according to the Wimborne & District News of that year. One of the main jobs of the "Romford Express" was to draw 20 ton loads to and from Southampton. Starting early in the morning the driver, Charles Churchill, travelled there and returned the next day.

All in all, the yard at Romford Mill was a very busy area with an engineering workshop, wheelwright and blacksmith as well as a sawmill. The original watermill was still working as a grist mill, preparing cattle feed for local farmers. There were fifteen steam engines each towing its own set of tackle comprising a threshing machine, elevator and caravan with a straw trusser at the rear.

The operators lived on the job during the week and worked as far away as Swanage, Salisbury and the Donhead villages near Shaftesbury. Threshing began in August for those farmers wanting the job done in the field whilst, as others stored crops in ricks during the winter, the threshers could continue until May when the engines returned to Romford for their summer overhaul. During the season two of Robert Thorne's sons collected the men at Saturday lunchtime and returned them to work at 5 a.m. on Monday to enable them to "get up steam" for the day's work. Whilst at home base, the engines were driven into the River Crane at Romford to take water on board and barrels were also filled and taken to the yard from the same source.

The heyday was in the 1930s but after that came a steady decline finally coming to an end in the 1960s after the invention of the combine harvester.

The sawmill, which also saw success in manufacturing pit props for the trenches in WWI, was razed to the ground by fire in the early 1920s and was replaced on new premises in Dewlands Road. The family moved from Romford Mill in 1934 to a large brick house named "The Coppice" on Station Road. By then, Robert had also bought the Crossroads Pottery from Fred Fry and owned parcels of land in both Verwood and Woodlands.

Robert Thorne Ltd. Timber Mills in Dewlands Road

"Robert Thorne Ltd." Became a limited company in 1944 with Robert, his wife Eva Jane neé Shearing and their five surviving children Clifford, Horace, Sidney, Blanche and Douglas as directors. Robert Thorne, a devout Methodist, died in 1946. Cliff had gone into farming but Sid, Horace and Doug continued the timber business, employing 60 men at one stage. Sid managed the sawmill, Horace, the woodlands and threshing whilst Doug took charge of the office. Timber was bought from estates such as Wimborne St. Giles, Crichel, Charborough Park and Breamore. The firm employed several hurdle makers who at one time produced 400 dozen hurdles a year for the Poundbury Sheep Fair which were sold off after the event.

When the remaining directors retired in 1998 the firm closed and the ground where it stood has now been developed as Old Sawmill Close.

OTHER INDUSTRIES

Returning from WWII, Verwood men were unable to resume work at the defunct brickworks and by then the only pottery remaining at the Crossroads employed a very limited staff. However, two unlikely saviours were to be found as this headline in the Wimborne and District News of 27th May 1950 proclaimed and is then continued in this extract and précis.

TWO DISUSED BRICKWORKS MEANT 'PAINT'

TO ONE MAN 'MUSHROOMS' TO ANOTHER

"This is a tale, not of two cities, but of two derelict brickworks and of the opportunities they represented to two men. Two similar brickworks, one at either end of Verwood, both made derelict upon the outbreak of the last war because their kilns were open fired and certain objectives of Nazi bombers, and two men with similar characteristics – initiative, determination, skilled experience and no fear of hard work. One man a brilliant chemist, whose life for years had begun and ended with the word "paint" and the other a man who for 20 years has lived and learnt "mushrooms."

FARROW & BALL "PREFERENCE PAINTS"

John (B.J.) Farrow was a London born chemist with a desire to make paint and convinced that he could. He came to Verwood and found just the right site in the Manor Brickworks on Black Hill. He recruited a friend Dick (R.M.) Ball, a local man from Sturminster Marshall who had been a P.O.W for five years but more importantly a skilled engineer. At this stage they had no capital so decided to raise some by manufacturing precipitated chalk which was in high demand for products such as toothpaste, face powder and rubber and latex goods. They had a drying shed and tons of chalk which was available locally through excavations such as for Corfe Mullen Water Works. Thus began two years of back breaking toil with the help of a lad until they had sufficient money to begin paint production.

Their first equipment consisted of three small paint making machines but even with these they were able to turn out paints of such high quality that no difficulty was experienced in marketing them. In fact demand soon exceeded supply so more capital was required to buy larger and better machinery with which to expand. They formed a limited company with Col. C. Chieveley Williams, O.B.E., T.D. as additional Director. More men were taken on and in 1949 they acquired the expertise of another Director in the form of Dr. E. Melling, M.Sc., Ph.D., a man recognised as one of the top three chemists in the paint trade. He and John Farrow had worked together during the war but it was only because Dr. Melling's health had forced him to move to the South that they were able to secure his services.

"Preference Paints" were supplied to prestigious firms and organisations such as the War Department, Air Ministry, Admiralty, Ford Motor Co., Richard Thomas Baldwins, Beric Ltd., Thorneycroft, County and Borough Councils etc. They exported to Iraq, Gibraltar, Malta and Egypt. "There probably isn't an Army, Air Force or Navy establishment in the southern half of England which has not used one or other of their paints." By this time they had a large, well-equipped laboratory as well as the manufacturing works.

Their tenure at the Manor Brickworks site came to a dramatic and abrupt end on 14th July 1967 when the paint factory was engulfed by fire. The firm has since moved to Uddens Industrial Estate at Ferndown and continues as one of the foremost and prestigious names in the industry worldwide. All this originated at a disused brickworks in post-war Verwood. The site was later taken over by Hampshire Tool Hire and is currently Bradford's Building Supplies. Just below on Black Hill in the Newtown Road direction was Stelrad which manufactured central heating radiators.

The spectacular fire at Farrow & Ball's Paint Factory on Black Hill 14th July 1967

Lesser Building Systems on the old Verwood Station Yard, now the site of Albion Way

OTHER INDUSTRIES

THE MUSHROOM FARM

Mr. and Mrs. W. Dunbar from northern England had spent many years in Canada where they learned the non-too-easy art of growing mushrooms. Times were bad there in 1928 when they managed to get a job with a man in this line of farming but within a year they had taken over the business when the owner went "bust". For the next nineteen years they studied, learned and built up a successful business.

In 1946, nostalgic for their homeland, they sold up and returned to look for a suitable site in which to take up their business in southern England. They finally decided on Verwood at a site on Dewlands Common but this was soon outgrown so, looking around for larger premises, the disused brickworks at Verwood Station presented a possibility. Here the old brick kilns were dark, easily heated in winter and cool in summer which were ideal conditions for this venture.

As in the case of the paint factory, capital was needed to upgrade their enterprise and so Mr. Dunbar became manager of Gotham Industries, the proprietor of which furnished the necessary capital on the understanding that Mr. Dunbar would act as manager for three years and then take over the business. So, in 1947 at an age when most people would think of retiring, Mr. & Mrs. Dunbar set to work. They had to clean out the brickworks, convert the kilns and, hardest of all, make living accommodation out of the derelict office building. This was almost falling down, the front door hung on a chain, there was no glass in the windows, no water, no light or any amenities. By 1950 it was spotlessly clean with a light and airy kitchen modelled as nearly as possible to Canadian standards.

Mr. Dunbar told the reporter "A.G.W." that since 1947 when they first started the continuous growing of mushrooms in the kilns, 100,000 lbs had been produced. Most of their trade was with the industrial Midlands and for this market they picked and despatched a regular 500 – 700 lbs each Monday. Most of the end of the week crop was disposed of locally in Bournemouth, Poole and around Verwood.

Mr. & Mrs. Dunbar took intense pride in their work and were rapidly becoming one of the largest mushroom producers in the country. Their ambition was to produce a ton of mushrooms per week at a price within reach of the bulk of the population.

The mushroom factory was next owned by the Lewington family who sold the site with associated buildings to Lesser's by whom the distinctive chimneys were demolished. People living in Pine View Road at the time remember watching them come tumbling down.

LESSER'S

This business came from Hounslow near London to the site of the former Station Yard in the 1960's, initially using the Station Master's house as their office, and was a major employer in the area until its Verwood premises closed in 1983. As well as their primary businesses the founding brothers also developed the Pine View estate area, naming Jessica Avenue after their mother.

At first they bought Jerry cans from the West Moors petrol depot and reconditioned them for resale. They then repaired Army pontoons before moving on to the manufacture of garden sheds which in turn led to the construction of prefabricated buildings exported all over Britain and other parts of the world.

One Verwood resident found himself in a makeshift passenger lounge and control building on an airstrip at Ras Gharib, Gulf of Suez, Egypt. It had certain familiarities and on inspecting the outside he found it was labelled "Made by Lesser of Verwood" just a few hundred yards from his home.

The long, flatbed lorries carrying these huge structures squeezed over the narrow railway bridge and were a familiar sight travelling down Station and Ringwood Roads, the vibrations alerting householders to their imminent approach.

BUSINESS AND TRADE

THE HIGGLERS

These itinerant hawkers took village goods such as pots, besoms and small farm produce for sale over a wide area. The earliest record of an earthenware dealer is to be found in the Poole Town accounts of 1731-2. "Half load of Earthenware Mr. Lawrince of Verwood .... 6d". This entry refers to cartage of pottery from Verwood to Poole for export.

The higglers usually loaded their wagons on Saturday afternoon ready for an early start on Monday morning, the intervening Sabbath being a sacred day when no work but the most essential could be contemplated. There were ructions on occasions when village lads, looking for amusement, led the horses up to the sandpit area, leaving the frustrated higglers to go and search for them before they could commence their journey.

One gentleman remembered accompanying his grandfather, leaving the village at 4 a.m. and travelling through the New Forest to reach Cadnam in time for breakfast. The "Sir John Barleycorn" was a favoured tavern at which to make the first stop on the journey in this direction. Carts would travel to Andover, Basingstoke and Salisbury with others going west to Warminster and even into Devon. The men would be many days on the road and not return until all the goods had been sold. After the advent of the railway, their trade doubled as they could send one cartload ahead and collect it when their first was empty.

Walter Fred "Pans" Brewer born 1879

James Bailey of Cherry Tree Cottage, Horton Way was one such dealer and in later years Walter Fred "Pans" Brewer is remembered as another as is Lot Oxford of Ringwood Road, a grandson of William Sims and Louisa Shearing. In 1891 the catalogue of those calling themselves, dealers and hawkers includes many familiar village names such as Beazeley, Brewer, King, Sims, Shearing, Trickett, Wareham and Roberts of Church Hill as well as Crutcher of Three Legged Cross. In this year there were twenty such who gave this as their profession on the census though others might have been somewhere out on the road.

In the early years of the twentieth century, one lady, Mrs. Emily Barrett of Three Legged Cross, advertised herself in Directories as a Higgler amongst local men of that trade.

THE SHOPS

Barrow Bros "The Verwood Stores" on Ringwood Road

Dedicated shopkeepers, grocers and bakers increased in number over the century, one such being Barrow's Stores in Ringwood Road where the purchase of numerous household items was made pleasant by the fragrant aroma of bread baking over hazelwood faggots.

John Barrow was born at Burley in the New Forest in 1852 but moved up to his wife Louisa Barker's county of Bedfordshire for many years. By 1901 they had moved south again to Verwood to establish a grocery store on the corner of Ringwood and Newtown Roads before

moving to a bakery and shop fronting Ringwood Road where some of their sons assisted them. Fred Barrow ran a delivery service with his horse "Old Tom" taking goods all over the scattered area and even obtained items to order such as medicines, not then available locally, from Ringwood which he would take to customers on his next round. There was little need to travel far for the staples of life apart from a trip into Ringwood Market on foot or by carrier cart. The shop later became a "Spar" grocery store, then for a short while a small shopping arcade and is now occupied by J.C.'s off-licence, convenience and video store above which the same gabled roof remains.

Into the twentieth century came many other useful grocers and general stores such as Henry's on the western corner of Ringwood and Newtown Roads, the site now occupied by a private house. It was then owned by Mr. Williams, Mr. Luxton and then Mr. Boswell who also provided a delivery service.

Mr. W.H. Rose, a Methodist local preacher, had a large store or emporium in Manor Road, just south of the chapels. He stocked groceries, drapery, hardware, boots and shoes and was an agency for Jones sewing machines. As you entered, the grocery was on the left and the drapers on the right. Mrs. Rose had charge of the clothes' department. Christine Stratton, née Henning, recalls the tins of biscuits and the drawers behind the counter containing spices. Sugar was weighed and put in a blue bag. Brushes and mops hung from the ceiling. The place smelled of polish. Olive Roberts, née Whitemore, remembers lovely ice-cream cakes and mock cream which you collected in a jam jar.

Eventually Miss Bell and Mrs. Coles took over and it became the Punch & Judy café, a very popular venue as a meeting place, for day to day meals and celebratory occasions. Hilary Joy, who was a waitress there, remembers the choice of cooked meals at mid-day. Soldiers from Blandford Camp who were learning to drive called in for meals, one group in the morning and another in the afternoon. Gerald and Ethel Froud were amongst those who had their wedding breakfast there. Congregational Chapel parties were held with Vera Reeks reciting monologues amongst other home grown entertainment. A great loss to the village occurred when fire destroyed the café in August 1968. It was never rebuilt for its former purpose but Brian Hall, a Verwood businessman, opened an estate agency on the site which is now the present Post Office next to A.W. Andrews, butcher.

Firemen on the scene at the Punch and Judy café blaze. It was then owned by Mrs. Grace Sims. As Verwood did not have its own Fire Brigade at that time the engine had to come from Cranborne or even further afield.

Further down Manor Road, on the opposite corner of Springfield Road to the garage, stood Goodfellow's General Store and Bakery. The bread ovens were at the back of the shop and home baked "dough cakes" were a very popular item. In the winter, a bucket of hot coals was brought from the bakery and put in the middle of the shop floor for heating. Later a "VG." store run by Mr. Len Faulkner, it is now the site of Harlees Fish and Chips.

BUSINESS AND TRADE

Jesse Shearing born 1820, who is credited with being the founder of Verwood Band, established Ringwood Road Stores sometime before 1881, his son Morris succeeding him. Morris, who died in 1948, left his sons Arthur the shop and Archie the bakery. His third son James, known as Jim, was given a piece of land adjacent to the shop which started himself and his son in the building trade. White Owl Stores stood on the corner of Newtown Road and Lake Roads on land which had once been Claylake Farm.

"Twitchen's" was a central grocery store on the south-western corner of Ringwood and Vicarage Roads adjoined by Lloyds Bank. The name became synonymous with this corner and "Meet you at Twitchens" is still used by some of the older folk.

The shop was later owned by Oliver Hill, then Pollards followed by Doughtys. It became Mace "Super-Fayre" run for many years by Mr. and Mrs. Everson and then the Geiger family before the opening of Safeway supermarket on 24th August 1982 changed Verwood's shopping habits for ever, leading to the demise of this and other useful outlets.

A youthful Matthew Reeks snapped by his father Ray whilst examining the announcement of the imminent opening of "Safeway Superstore"

West of the grocery shop, facing the Recreation Ground, was a brick dwelling with integral shop housing John Thomas "Jack" Blake's Outfitters. Jack's wife Daisy was the daughter of Sidney Bailey and Thirza Turner Shearing, both from long established Verwood families. Like other close-knit communities, the ramifications of the genealogical history of the inhabitants would take up several volumes! Daisy long outlived Jack, reaching the age of 102 and was cheerful to the last when spending her last years at a Nursing Home in the New Forest. The shop later became "Chandler Wine" Off-Licence but has since been demolished.

Next to that, immediately after WWII, a small hut contained Roy King's radio and cycle shop. He also operated the petrol pumps on the forecourt of the adjacent Central Garage though later the Garnham family took over this filling station. The garage building itself housed "Gull Enterprises" who made outboard engines. When Eddie Armsdon's "Verwood Engineering", a transport and plant hire business, took over the garage premises around 1953, the small shop became his office with Margaret Hudson presiding as Transport Manager. Beyond was a pond behind which stood the Gas Showrooms in an area somewhat grandly known as "The Square". This was run by Fred Trout and Stan Prince who used it as a base and for storing equipment. Stan remembers having to cycle to Ferndown to collect his 11/11d. wages. The Crossroads Pottery and Ernie Whitehorn's cycle shop continued this row of businesses towards Manor Road as far as the Congregational Chapel.

On the opposite side of the road stood Shearing's cycle repair shop and garage with the forge behind on land later used as their motor repair works. The large, square brick building on the corner was a double house built in 1904. Fred Shearing lived in the half nearest the garage and later his son Ron lived in the other. On the west side of the garage stood another brick house inhabited by Danny McDougal, a Special Constable in charge of blackout arrangements during the war. He was a very large man capable of scaring anyone who dared to show so much as a chink of light. His wife sold bric-a-brac and jewellery from a wooden shed in the front garden.

On this side of the road stood other wooden huts selling a variety of goods over time. Harold Ferrett then Ernie Nicklen sold wet and fried fish on certain days of the week. Mr. Carr sold confectionery and ice cream, Miss Price "Arts and Crafts". Opposite, in a shed on the north side Mr. Gilhooly, a man blinded in the First World War, made "cocoa mats".

On that side of the road too, a little further west, was a Chemist's shop built before the Second World War. Mr. Stone was the pharmacist after leaving a smaller shop in The Parade and in May 1946 it was taken over by Mr. Hubert Baker and family. It is later remembered as belonging to John Gallagher until his retirement when it was taken over briefly by the Lloyds pharmacy chain before they moved into the new surgery complex in 2000.

The complex of shops on the north-west corner of the Crossroads in or around 1925
whilst Mr. Austin still held the newsagency but after Mabel Rose Whitemore had opened her
China, Glass and Hardware store which later became a wet and cooked fish shop.
Far right is Mr. Bill Smith's shoe shop, later that of Arthur and Iris Bailey, eventually "Paula's Place"

The distinctive three-sided building on the north-west corner of the Crossroads was built by Job Brewer in the early twentieth century. The first Newsagent was Francis Austin, a retired policeman from London. Arthur Hopkins, manager of the Brick and Tile Yard, then bought it around 1926 as a business for his unmarried daughter Nellie, whose principles would not allow her to sell cigarettes or open on Sundays. Even up to the 1960s the shop would never open on a Sunday so a newsagent from Ringwood would bring a stall to sell papers outside. In earlier days it also contained a lending library and later in addition to stationery, papers, magazines and tobacco products it sold basic groceries, novelty goods, children's toys and was a lottery outlet. It stayed in the same family hands for eighty-one years right up to 2005 when Julian King, a Hopkins descendant and the then current proprietor, retired.

Centre stood Mabel Whitemore's hardware store. This lady obviously inherited her entrepreneurial talents being the daughter of Harry Brewer of the Manor Brickworks and niece of his brother Job. She also operated a motor-bike and sidecar round to Woodlands, Cranborne, Alderholt and around the village selling items such as soaps and polishes. About 1925 she and her husband, Leonard, started a printing business in their front room next to the shop and continued, with a treadle press, in a wooden hut, built for this purpose, on the other side. About 1939 the hardware store moved to a wooden building further up Edmondsham Road, now the Fayrewood Gallery, with the expanded printing works in stables at the rear. In later years Leo Roberts, husband of the Whitemore's daughter Olive, became a well-known and loved Verwood figure presiding over the press and producing posters, leaflets, handbooks, headed notepaper and countless other useful stationery items.

BUSINESS AND TRADE

When Mabel Whitemore's shop moved to Edmondsham Road, the original premises came into the hands of Ernie Nicklen who sold wet and cooked fish. In 1950 it was bought by David Day and placed under the management of Mr. and Mrs. Coombes who were married on a Saturday, had their honeymoon on Sunday and started work there on Monday morning. As Mr. Coombes had to travel to the fish market in the early hours, his wife had to be an early riser also in order to attend to the needs of the shop and later of their children.

In the adjacent wooden hut an Electrical business was started by Len Halfacre, followed by Mr. Wilkinson and then Fred and Olive Bailey in 1954/5 who displayed a TV in the window, a washing machine in the shop and had their workshop behind. Fred then moved to the disused Crossroads Pottery building after the decorating firm of Cox and Guy vacated the premises. Here he took charge of radio and television being joined by his brother Maurice and by Mike Hudson who looked after washing machines. On 25th March 1960 the Restynge House on Ringwood Road was sold by the church and bought by the Bailey family who expanded their business with a showroom entitled "Television House", selling these increasingly popular items of home entertainment as well as many other electrical items. The Restynge House was demolished in 1989 to make way for an enlarged version to include a new showroom as well as other shops and offices. Today, under new ownership, it still retains the name of its founders "Baileys of Verwood".

Returning to Edmondsham Road, on the site of the Fayrewood Court flats once stood Mr. Bill Smith's boot and shoe repairer shop. A disabled man, he used a tricycle to travel in from Cranborne to work at a hut on the site. The landowner, Job Brewer, thought this too much for him so built him a house and workshop there. Bill left the business to Arthur and Iris Bailey who had been respectively his apprentice and housekeeper before their marriage. Arthur took charge of the repairs whilst Iris, neé Cabell, looked after the sales. Service was such that if a particular model or size was not in stock it would be ordered by telephone and arrive at Verwood station later that same afternoon. In latter years it became "Paula's Place" a very useful clothes shop which also stocked items of children's footwear.

THE PARADE

A variety of small shops with living quarters behind and above. Now occupied by service outlets such as estate agents, a bank and travel agent with other businesses on the first floor. No doubt this is a sign of the changing times in the retail trade.

Back on Ringwood Road, "The Parade" was built after World War I under the Government subsidy scheme. Brothers Job and Harry Brewer owned half each. Originally they were private houses with a wicket fence enclosing small front gardens. Harry extended his frontage to form a shop which his wife Emma Rose ran as "The Verwood Bon Marche" which although sometimes seen in advertisements with a continental accent over the final "é" was never pronounced in the French fashion. This was a very useful haberdashery shop which sold wool, ladies' outfits and household linen. If your requirement was not it stock, it was ordered. Prices always ended in ¾d with pins, buttons or wool being offered as change. In the 1960s until closure it was owned by Mrs. Shearing, a descendant of the Brewer family, and staffed by the Mouland sisters. Purchases were accompanied by Green Shield Stamps, a popular discount collecting scheme at the time.

BUSINESS AND TRADE

At the far end of The Parade from Bon Marche was Shutler & Denham "Nurserymen, Seedsmen and Florists" of the Cross Roads Nurseries who had greenhouses at the rear to supply their produce. The shop sold greengrocery and flowers including the making up of funeral wreaths and also confectionery. Others at various times were Wilfred Chubb, barber, with Mrs. Chubb's ladies' salon above, Mr. E. S. Stone, Chemist and Optician, as well as Verwood Library under the benign despotism of Miss Jasper who had no hesitation in advising clients, especially younger ones, what they could or could not read whilst firmly stamping on those who let their books run overdue.

The Verwood butcher's shop was originally in Ringwood Road in the building currently occupied by the Indian Palace restaurant. Mr. F. C. Cobb is the earliest remembered followed by Hammonds and then Shakles. A later butcher, Mr. Edwin Thomas Legg, was a very religious man who placed bible texts in the window, amusing the villagers greatly when "Worthy the Lamb that was slain for us" appeared one day.

Bill Andrews from Christchurch bought the business in the mid 1950s with his brother Dan installed as Manager. In 1957 he sold the shop to Dan and opened his own newly built premises in Manor Road "A. W. Andrews" which celebrated its "Golden Jubilee" in 2007. Bill and his wife Audrey retired in 1986, handing over the business to their son Billy and daughter Janet who had long assisted in the family firm. When Dan and his wife Joyce retired in 1988 that shop closed. Their daughter Hazel, also an integral member of her parents' butchery, joined her cousins at the Manor Road premises but has since moved on.

THE NEW INN

Priddle & Franklin's sweet shop in the old New Inn on Church Hill, the white building on the right. Looking down to Margards Lane, here erroneously called "St. Margaret's"

In the early twentieth century, Mr. Reginald Franklin was the proprietor of a very popular sweet shop in the premises previously occupied by the New Inn. One farthing would buy aniseed balls, beans or popcorn and also sherbet tubes. When the shop door was opened, a bell rang to warn Mr. Franklin who could be in the coach house or stables from where he ran a horse and trap taxi service. Verwood people remember the sense of occasion when their parents hired Mr. Franklin to take them to or from the station. Mrs. Franklin's stepmother, Mrs. Eliza Priddle, known as "Granny Franklin" helped out in the shop wearing a lace bonnet which must have added an air of old fashioned quaintness to proceedings.

Another well remembered sweet shop was Mrs. Lillian Bowden's confectionery, small grocery and haberdashery store in the central part of the former Restynge House. She was a niece of Mr. Franklin, her mother's brother. Her parents Christopher and Elizabeth Grace had been the first caretakers of the Restynge House when it was built in 1907 as the Anglican Church Hall and meeting place, a role later taken over by her husband Frank.

One rather surprising shop belonged to the potter Meshech Sims at his house in Burnbake Road where he sold sweets, cigarettes, tobacco and lead soldiers!

An addition to the established public houses, the Albion at the station and the Travellers Rest at Three Legged Cross, came with the Monmouth Ash in Manor Road in the mid twentieth century. This had been Edwin Charles Dibben's Beer Retail and Off-Licence until taken over and converted into a pub by Hall and Woodhouse Brewery. By then the Heathpoult at Eastworth and the New Inn had long since ceased trading.

Another very popular feature of Verwood life was the weekly Auction Market. On Ringwood Road, at the entrance to what is now Strathmore Drive was a five bar gate leading into the property of Fred "Pans" Brewer. There was a mud walled shed in the grounds used for storing straw and the horse and cart. This shed was cleared on Auction Day. In the early 1930s Welch & Lock were the Auctioneers and Fred Brewer carried items in his horse and cart and latterly in a lorry. Behind the shed, trestle tables were put up so that rabbits, fowls, chickens and small animals in cages could be placed on them.

In the late 1930s David and Mary Wilson took over the market. Mary Butler, an Edmondsham farmer's daughter, had entered her future father-in-law's office of estate agents and auctioneers on leaving school in 1938. Whilst her husband was away on war service in 1944 she conducted her first public auction, just before her 21st birthday, a role she made very much her own for many years to come.

Initially they worked at the Ringwood Road site but moved to "Amberley" in Manor Road which had originally been a poultry farm. A small shed beside the house was used as an insurance office and became Verwood's first estate agency. A large poultry shed behind was converted into an auction room, Fred Brewer continuing to act as the goods transporter. Anything and everything came under Mrs. Wilson's hammer – garden produce, flowers, cakes, animals, prams and furniture to name but a few of the countless items sold over the years.

Three Legged Cross had its own outlets. Mr. and Mrs. Gregory's store and Post Office at the junction of Verwood and Horton Roads was famous for its appetizing smell of baking bread whilst Mrs. Gregory made wonderful cakes. The Gregorys later moved up to Verwood Post Office, taking over from the long established postmaster there, Mr. Frank Dowland. This corner shop was later owned by long standing local, district and county Councillor William Wells and family before being demolished in 1983 and flats built on the site. James Henry Hammond had a shop in Church Road in 1939 which was later taken over by the Dykes before being owned by the Webster family when it sold general groceries, Horton's ice cream, paraffin and charged batteries before closing about 1975.

Ye Olde Greye Cottage. Three Legged Cross, Dorset   No

YE OLDE GREYE COTTAGE

The Misses Margaret and Edith Franks were hostesses at this guest house and tearoom on the Horton Road. They are also remembered for selling ice creams to passers by. The building, later converted into the Capercailzie Restaurant, was demolished to build Greycot Close in the 1980s.

"Mace" was one of Verwood's supermarkets before 1982 and as with many local shops, utilised the downstairs room of a house. There was no such thing as late night shopping in those days. You bought what you needed before 5.30 p.m. and definitely nothing on Sundays!

MACE "SUPER-FAYRE"
On the corner of Ringwood and Vicarage Roads

The old Crossroads Pottery housed a variety of enterprises between 1952 and 1996 – Tea Rooms and Craft Shop, Decorators, Electricals, Plumbers and Hardware Store. In the latter you bought screws, nails and other items in the exact number you required rather than being obliged to buy a whole packet. The double yellow lines indicate a time when you could drive through this shortcut between Manor and Ringwood Roads.

THE POTTERS WHEEL ON MANOR WAY
Now Verwood Heathland Heritage Centre

Webster's Stores was one of the main sources of groceries and other useful items for the people of Three Legged Cross in the mid twentieth century. It stood towards the north eastern end of Church Road but has since been demolished and replaced by housing. Fortunately since then, Three Legged Cross has acquired other useful shopping outlets.

WEBSTERS STORES

Verwood Post Office in Vicarage Road. The postmaster, Mr. Frank Dowland commissioned many scenes of early 20th century Verwood for which we have reason to be grateful. The men cycled or walked many miles over the heathland to deliver mail to a scattered community. Note the gas street lamp right.

Left: The Post Office extended and run in the 1970s by Geoff and Denny Frost who obtained a licence to sell "Galt" toys. The pillar box was the first of its kind in Verwood and presaged its growing status as a town. Extended, it now contains a Florist, Solicitor and Optician.

"Chandler Wine" Off-Licence opposite the Recreation Ground was formerly John T. Blake's Outfitters. The small hut used to be Roy King's Radio and Cycle Shop where he charged accumulators and also had a jigsaw puzzle cutting machine. The adjacent Central Garage housed a variety of businesses after WWII. A convenience store and its car park now cover this whole site.

THE ALBION HOTEL

Above: The Albion Hotel, built as the Station Inn in the 1860s. Here shown in its original form with a heart shaped decoration of white Ebblake brick. To the left are the stables whilst a row of fire buckets hangs on the station fence. The foreground is now the Beer Garden.

Below, Alan, Wesley, Alec and Monsell Shearing raise their glasses in a toast whilst Lily stands between as they leave the premises on 30th July 1976. Wesley and Lily were a very popular couple who ran the Inn for 47 years. They had a long standing family association with it too as Wesley's grandfather, John Wesley Beckingham, had been one of the early licensees whilst Lily's father had later been another well-known landlord, Samuel Parker.

BUSINESS AND TRADE

In addition to the retail outlets were many self-employed tradesmen and delivery services. One such was Mr. Teddy Roberts of Church Hill who sold the unlikely combination of fish and paraffin on his rounds. Below and on the following page are some examples of the facilities available in Verwood in the early to mid twentieth century.

VALENTINE REEKS – COAL MERCHANT

SHEARING'S DAIRY

CECIL KING - HAULIER

Valentine Reeks lived and had his depot close to the station in the lane behind the Albion Hotel on the north side of the Cranborne Road.

Tom Steele, Lot Budden and F. Savage were also Coal Merchants as had been Henry Charles Hopkins, brother of Arthur of the Tile Works. Arthur and Charles had both come to Verwood just before 1891 as Brickmakers.

Ira Henning who lived at "Penarth", Manor Road was the Local Agent for Messrs. Bryer Ash Ltd., Wessex Coal Merchants.

Cousins Reg and Ted Shearing delivering milk in the 1920s for their uncle Charles Shearing of Dewlands Common. Reg who was the brother of Eric of the Crossroads Garage, later took over the business. The round continued at least to the 1960s but by then deliveries were on motor bike and sidecar.

Ken Brewer, son of "Pans", another milk supplier had his depot behind Barrow's Stores on Ringwood Road.

Cecil King was a haulier at Three Legged Cross in the days when lorries had taken over from horse and cart. He delivered pots and besoms. Fred "Pans" Brewer sometimes used Mr. King to carry his goods around the area.

BUSINESS & TRADE

TOM PRIOR – BOOT MAKER & REPAIRER

THE DORSET FARMERS LTD

MISS EMILY PALMER WITH HER DONKEY CART

Tom Prior had a wooden hut in Ringwood Road. He was one of several boot makers and repairers, a vital service in a country area with rough, unmade roads.

Lot Oxford told a story of his grandfather taking him to Ringwood to buy a pair of "Watertites" which the young lad proceeded to try out with disastrous effects in a pool on the common. Even worse was to come when he attempted to repair the damage by putting them secretly in the oven. Grandfather's wrathful reaction to the charred remains was not something Lot was likely to forget in a hurry!

The Dorset Farmers Verwood depot in the Station Goods Yard. This was a co-operative organisation supplying feedstuffs and the like to farms throughout the area. Left to right: Charles Trowbridge, Peter Reeks and Jim Pearce.

Emily Palmer was the daughter of William, the owner of Somerley Brickyard at Ebblake. Here seen outside Ebblake House, the family's home.

She was a familiar sight around the village with her donkey cart which she also used to take into the New Forest to transport heather which her brothers had earlier walked there to cut.

THE SOCIAL SCENE

Although there was never much money to spare, Verwood did not lack means of entertainment or social occasions. Haymaking and Harvest celebrations, Bonfire Night, Church Festivals and the annual December Fair on Church Hill agreeably punctuated the annual calendar. For the Fair, Mr. Teddy Roberts, who lived nearby, had several sideshows including a donkey target which kicked when hit in the middle with an air rifle. Mrs. Roberts was at hand with her sweet stall, a piece of three cornered rock being given to every contestant successful or not. After the Fair lapsed, Verwood Carnival was soon to take its place and has been a fixture ever since. Such was its popularity in the mid twentieth century that coach companies ran excursions from as far afield as Bournemouth for the day and extra trains were laid on.

A walk or ride to Ringwood Market, or even Wimborne, gave a change of scene and an opportunity to view and purchase goods not available locally. For the men, there were the public houses or more soberly the Restynge House which hosted various activities and contained a Reading Room without the necessity of buying alcoholic drinks.

Several groups, especially attached to the churches, provided a social outlet for the ladies of the community once their daily tasks were done. In addition there was the communal spirit of the Women's Institute.

The children enjoyed occasional treats and picnics and in the early twentieth century an annual excursion, sometimes to Bournemouth, when the pleasurable journey by horse drawn charabanc took most of the day with a bare half hour to frolic on sand and in sea.

Higher Moor Pool on Boveridge Heath above Noon Hill Road

Nearer at hand much enjoyment could be had from makeshift swimming pools on Boveridge Heath. Two of these were called "Bunny" and "Higher Moor". The pool at Does Hatches, on the River Crane was also used for this purpose. Many children learned to swim there and as late as August 1943 the Council School Log Book records that "this afternoon, the children were paraded for bathing at Does Hatches". This pool is now part of Crane Valley Golf Club.

Children could sail on logs of wood or any impromptu vessel such as a tin bath on the village ponds. One such was where the Monmouth Ash now stands with another on the opposite side of Manor Road on the southern corner of Church Hill. There was also a large duck pond opposite Does Farm in Dewlands Road.

Verwood Cricket Team outside the Restynge House in 1912
Rev. Claud Brown at centre back and Samuel Parker, Licensee of the Albion far right
Sadly not all of these young men returned from the First World War

Sporting activities also enjoyed to the full included football, cricket, hockey, tennis and bowls, all of which flourished from the early twentieth century. One of the keenest adherents of the game of cricket was Rev. Claud Brown who even in blind old age had to have all the first class scores read out to him daily by his somewhat reluctant granddaughter. In his heyday, he travelled to away matches in the seat of honour atop the beer barrel and it has been suggested that his nickname should have been "Slogger" as, although he didn't always connect, when he did the ball had to reach the boundary. At this time the team's home ground was on a field at Verwood Farm, kindly made available by the Standfield family. Fittingly, it is now part of Emmanuel School playing fields.

After WWI when the Recreation Ground was inaugurated many of Verwood's sporting activities and outdoor social events too place there and most transferred to Potterne Park in 1986 when these playing fields were made available to the community by East Dorset District Council. They were managed by VADACSAR, a successor to Verwood Sports Council, as was the Leisure Centre opened in October 1982 for which the Association had lobbied hard and eventually successfully for one to be built in conjunction with Safeway supermarket. This organization is now known as Verwood Community Association.

Children enjoyed their own version of these sporting activities. A boys' football team was ably coached in the 1950s and 60s by Mrs. Reg Trickett. Rossgarth Football Club, another youth team, which is still very active, was started in the mid twentieth century and played for many years on a field off Ringwood Road belonging to Mr. Reg Day.

Young people also enjoyed such organized activities as Scouts and Guides from the very earliest days of the movements. The Church of England Scouts were led by the Vicar's son, Audley Brown, whilst those of the Chapel were under the charge of Rev. Morley Worsam, Pastor from 1914 to the early 1920s. Several groups of Scouts met in a small upstairs room at the Crossroads Pottery before having their own dedicated headquarters.

THE SOCIAL SCENE

The Guides were fortunate to have living in the village Miss Lorna Limpus, daughter of Admiral and Lady Limpus who lived at "Cartref" in Manor Road. Miss Limpus had been a Scout before the girls' section was formed and was a personal friend of Lady Baden-Powell who came to visit her when duties allowed. Miss Limpus, who died in 1971 at the age of 77, was much revered amongst the community and very active in promoting Verwood's interests in all spheres. Both Scouts and Guides now have modern headquarters on Potterne Hill, the latter being dedicated to Mrs. Paddy Reeks, a long time Verwood and District Guide Leader who promoted the new building but sadly died before its completion.

Early Verwood Girl Guides

Entertainments and concerts became enjoyable events. Mr. W. G. Stickland, a West Moors Estate Agent during his working life, transformed himself out of hours into a skilled and popular magician "The Wessex Wizard" to the great enjoyment and mystification of all. Amateur Dramatics has long played a part in Verwood life and has since been joined by the Pantomime Society along with various acting and dancing opportunities for young and old.

There was a small Conservative and Unionist Hall, known as "The Village Hall" on the corner of the Crossroads at Verwood which played host to many social events of this kind but was replaced by the Memorial Hall in 1959 after many years of fund raising. Three Legged Cross Village Hall was built in 1927 on land given by Lord Shaftesbury for that purpose, again after many fund raising events, and is still a hive of various activities. After WWI, The Royal British Legion Club in Moorlands Road added to the social outlets both for members and for functions.

Today there are a host of special interest clubs, sports teams and activities for all age groups, too numerous to mention individually. Verwood was twinned with Champtoceaux, Brittany in 1984 at the suggestion of Manitou (UK) Ltd who had moved into Ebblake Industrial Estate and had links with the French town. Champtoceaux's German twin town, Liederbach am Taunus, was then also twinned with Verwood in 1992. The Twinning Association promotes international friendship and cultural exchange. A great accolade was achieved in 2006 when Verwood and Three Legged Cross were the only area in the U.K. to be awarded the European Flag of Honour.

The Rustic Fayre, a charitable event as is the Carnival, was started in 1982 by the Community Association on Reg Day's field in Ringwood Road but is now organized by Verwood Rotary Club and held on August Bank Holiday Monday at Potterne Park. Other social events such as the Carnival, Flameburst Firework Display, Soundburst Youth Music Festival and the annual opening venue of Jay Miller's Circus are presently held on Adrian Wareham's field off Crane Drive, nicknamed "The Fuzzy Bit".

THE SOCIAL SCENE

No mention of entertainment and social activities would be complete without that of the Verwood Band. The ensemble has a long, continuous history, the first known being the Temperance Band believed to have been started by Jesse Shearing in about 1864. The first recorded report is of the band leading a procession to the Queen Victoria Monument in nearby Woodlands in celebration of the monarch's Golden Jubilee in 1887. They rehearsed in the Chapel Schoolrooms or even in the open air, their uniform consisting of a pillbox hat and a satchel in which to keep their music.

Verwood Temperance Band

By the 1920s the band wore flat peaked caps and charabancs were used to travel further afield to contests. During this era they were strongly associated with the Black Hill Brickworks. By this time they were rehearsing in the wooden TOC H Hut in Moorlands Road, behind the Recreation Ground. This had been given by Mr. Sidney Palmer, owner of Verwood Sandpits, on condition that the band, of which he was a supporter and benefactor, could use it twice a week. They continued to use this hut, which also hosted wedding receptions and other social activities, until 1994 when a purpose built Band Hall was built on the same site. Their ability was such that from the 1930s to 1970s they were known as Verwood Prize Band, reverting to Verwood Band for a short time before adopting the present name of Verwood Concert Brass to reflect a more modern image. In addition to the main Band, a Training Band consists of juniors and those of more mature age who have decided to take up an instrument later in life.

As well as participating in nationwide contests, the band holds concerts and gives other performances throughout the area as well as leading the procession for the annual Verwood Carnival and playing at many local events. They also act as Town Ambassadors on twinning occasions both home and abroad. No Christmas would be complete without their seasonal renditions at various points around the town. Verwood can be justly proud of the tradition they have created and upheld to the present day.

"The Hub", a state of the art venue funded by East Dorset District Council opened in March 2007. The main hall is named "The Merryfield Theatre" in honour of actor Buster Merryfield, "Uncle Albert" in the BBC TV series "Only Fools and Horses" who lived in Verwood for several years. When he died in 1999 his co-stars, David Jason and Nicholas Lyndhurst, led the funeral mourners at St. Michael and All Angels parish church.

On 9th July 2006 M.P. Chris Chope officially launched Verwood's own local Radio Station, Forest FM 92.3, pioneered by Steve Saville, with its studio sited on the Ebblake Industrial Estate. This has truly brought the art of entertainment into the 21st century.

THE SOCIAL SCENE

Maypole Dancing in the early 20th century

LIVING WHIST

An early twentieth century pageant held in the large rear garden of "Oaklands" now No. 72 Manor Road. Children were dressed as playing cards and dealt by the adults as in a real game. Courtly dancing provided additional entertainment.

**AUBREY BARROW
WITH
LIONEL JEFFRIES**

Amateur Dramatics or the "AmDrams" have always played an important part in Verwood entertainment. Lionel Jeffries became President of the Society and is seen left in company with Aubrey Barrow, a leading light in local dramatic and musical productions. Born in London in 1926, Lionel spent several of his childhood years in Verwood, attending Queen Elizabeth School at Wimborne. During a distinguished career in later life he starred as Grandpa Potts in "Chitty Chitty Bang Bang" and directed the 1970 version of "The Railway Children".

Above in lighthearted mood, the Youth Group enacts the Pantomime "Cinderella" with a Wimborne & Rural District Dustcart taking the place of the fairytale coach. Pictured are Paul Eyres, Bill Walbridge, Ray Reeks and Joe Shearing.

Home grown entertainment groups still thrive in the community.

The above photograph shows those taking part in the first organized outing from the Traveller's Rest Inn at Three Legged Cross.

In the 1930s, charabanc trips were a very popular annual outing for clubs and societies. Various south coast seaside resorts were usually chosen including Weymouth, Swanage, Southsea, Bognor Regis and even as far afield as Eastbourne.

THE WOMEN'S SOCIAL HOUR
Garden Meeting held 21ˢᵗ June 1932 at "The Anchorage", Lake Road, Verwood
home of Reverend & Mrs. Cannell, parents of Dennis, Nora (who became Mrs. Poole) and five other children

Names attributed above are

BACK ROW: 1. Mrs. Grout (President) 2. Unidentified 3. Mrs. Winnie Shearing née Brewer 4. Mrs. Gilhooly 5. Mrs. James 6. Miss Norah Standfield 7. Mrs. Augustus Thorne 8. Mrs. Rose Ferrett 9. Mrs. Oliver Thorne 10. Unidentified

3ᴿᴰ ROW: 1. Mrs. Cannell 2. Unidentified 3. Mrs. John Morgan 4. Mrs. Sidney Palmer 5. Mrs. Froud 6. Mrs. Fred Brewer with ? 7. Mrs. Orman 8. Unidentified 9. Mrs. Giles Sims 10. Mrs. Clifford Barrow 11. Miss Mary Thorne 12. Mrs. Martin Ferrett 13. Unidentified

2ᴺᴰ ROW: 1. Mrs. Pearl Reeks née Brewer 2. Mrs. Fred Shearing 3. Mrs. Flemington 4. Mrs. Sanger 5. Unidentified. 6. Mrs. Charles Reeks. 7. Mrs. Agnes Thorne née Reeks with Ken 8. Mrs. Arthur Bailey 9. Mrs. Nell Waters 10. Mrs. Anne Thorne.

FRONT ROW: 1. Miss Nellie Hopkins 2. Mrs. Charlie Hopkins 3. Mrs. Raymond Heckford. 4. Child Heckford? 5. Child B 6. Child C 7. Child D 8. Rita Oxford 9. Mrs. Lottie Oxford 10. Mrs. Brown

The Minutes of the Women's Social Hour tell us that "On Wednesday January 26ᵗʰ 1928 a Drawing Room Meeting was held at Mrs Grout's house to consider the advisability of starting a women's meeting. It was attended by nineteen ladies. After due consideration it was arranged to commence a "Women's Social Hour", the meetings to be held fortnightly on a Tuesday afternoon at quarter to three and held alternately at the Wesleyan & Congregational Schoolrooms. It was agreed that members pay 2d each meeting and that a cup of tea etc. be provided."

The organisation thrived, with increased membership, Mrs. Grout remaining President for thirty years. As well as the fortnightly meetings, a Christmas party and summer Garden party were held with missionary meetings and an annual outing to a wide variety of destinations across the south, increasing in scope as transport became more modernised.

Similar activities and charitable enterprises were arranged by the Mothers' Union for those attending the Parish Church. The Women's Institute has long been a democratic organization with branches in both Verwood and Three Legged Cross. Verwood Wives' Group remains a popular, independent social club over which Mrs. Ruth Bussey presided for many years.

THE SOCIAL SCENE

VERWOOD CONGREGATIONAL CHURCH BAZAAR c. 1950

BACK ROW: 1. Maurice Brewer   2. Mrs. Joyce Cartwright   3. Pamela Cartwright   4. Mrs. Grace Seymour
5. Mrs. Waterhouse 6. Mrs. Vera Reeks   7. Miss Maud Haskell 8. Harold Ferrett
9. Mrs. Beatrice Lockyer   10. Mrs. Stickland   11. Alf Lockyer

MIDDLE ROW: 1. Mrs. Dora Harley   2. Unidentified 3. Mrs. Gladys Williams (wife of Rev. A. W. Williams)

FRONT ROW: 1. Mrs. Greenwood 2. Mrs. Lily Young 3. Dolly Parker 4. Lily Brewer
5. Mrs. Bennett (became Mrs. Basil Joy)   6. Dorrie Haskell

VERWOOD PRIZE BAND IN THE 1930s
They wore navy uniforms with silver and black braid

BACK ROW: 1. Jack Day 2. Jim Bailey 3. Charlie Brewer 4. Herby Brewer 5. Alan Case 6. Cyril Trickett

MIDDLE ROW: 1. Tom Spencer 2. George Daniels 3. Charlie Seaton   4. Ivor Keevil 5. Eddie Haskell   6. Bill Green
7. Ralph Thorne 8. Jack Sims 9. George Sims

FRONT ROW: 1. Ted Shearing 2. Redmond Seaton 3. Jim Haskell 4. Sidney Shutler (Director and Conductor)
5. Sidney Palmer 6. Jim Shearing 7. Jim Ferrett

THE SOCIAL SCENE

Scouting was available to Verwood boys from the earliest days of the movement. The vicar's son, Audley Brown, led the Church troop. On Scout Sunday, the choirboys used to walk in their uniforms to Three Legged Cross to sing Evensong at All Saints.

Left: Rev. Worsley Morsam, the Independent Minister with the Chapel troop "on manoeuvres" at Crab Orchard.

Above: A thriving Youth Group was attached to the Methodist Church. On 22nd October 1955 they held their 25th Anniversary Ball at the Hall on the corner of the Crossroads. Guest of Honour was the famous athlete, Chris Chataway, a participant in the record breaking first four minute mile the previous year. He presented Gordon Thorne with a travel clock as he was about to leave for National Service.

Below: Former Youth Group Members reunited in 1987 at Verwood Leisure Centre

Verwood Youth Group topically reenacts the conquest of Mount Everest in 1953, complete with Yeti, for the celebrations of the Coronation of Queen Elizabeth II.

The 1968 Carnival Queen, Hilary Manlove, being regally transported along Manor Road. The beautiful horses were owned and led by Mr. Tom Sampson of Harbridge.

Three Legged Cross celebrates the Silver Jubilee of Queen Elizabeth II in 1977 with a Fancy Dress Parade.

1st Prize: John Forster

2nd Prize: Terri Shearing

3rd Prize: Coral Hale

VERWOOD FOOTBALL CLUB – 1922-1923
In front of the old Pavilion on the Recreation Ground.

BACK ROW: 1. Fred Willis   2. Job Brewer   3. Keith Barrow   4. ? Petty   5. Maurice Ferrett   6. George Thorne
7. Ted Sandy   8. Fred Scammel senior   9. Frank Brewer

MIDDLE ROW: 1. Ernie Northeast   2. Sidney Bailey   3. Ginger Wilcox   4. Ken Brewer

FRONT ROW: 1. Norman Barrett   2. Wesley Shearing   3. Clifford Barrow   4. ? Hiscock (from Gotham)
5. George "Drummer" Brewer (from Three Legged Cross)

YOUTH FOOTBALL TEAM c. 1960

BACK ROW: 1. Jimmy Hawker 2. Gary Scammell 3. Ian Atyeo 4. John Barrow 5. Dennis Barrow 6. Ken Guy
7. Geoffrey Rimmer 8. David Dommett 9. Mervyn Coombs

FRONT ROW: 1. Neil Atyeo 2. Frank Day 3. Arthur Barrow 4. Stephen Day 5. Ted Cox, Journalist & Local Historian
6. Mrs. Reg Trickett (Coach) 7. Rev. A. W. Williams, Congregational Minister 8. Stephen Prince 9. Paul Barrow

WAR AND SERVICE

In the early days, few Verwood men appear to have joined the Armed Forces through choice. Amongst those known are Dan Sims, born 1844 to William Sims and Louisa Shearing of Ringwood Road and brother to potters Robert and Seth, who became a Royal Marine. He was uncle to Lot Oxford the higgler whose boyhood recollections were of a very smart man who wore a beautiful red coat with bright buttons. He remembered him as a very kind uncle who, when on leave, used to give Lot 6d to clean his buttons and boots a task the boy no doubt performed with pride. Mark Bailey, born 1851 at Cherry Tree Cottage, Horton Way, son of James Bailey and Jane Hatch became a seaman in the Royal Navy. Herbert Bailey born 1873 at Mannington near Three Legged Cross, son of Job Bailey and Sophia Knowlton, joined the Royal Artillery, serving in the Boer War and in India where he died at the age of 42 being buried at Rawalpindi Cemetery now in Pakistan.

The First World War was of course to change all that with Verwood men deployed in many unfamiliar theatres of action across the globe. For some it may have been an initial excitement to be taken away from mundane jobs until the awful reality of bloodshed set in. A total of forty names was recorded on the churchyard War Memorial though several of these came from West Moors which was at that time in the ecclesiastical parish of Verwood. Both the Dyer and Dowland families lost three sons each. Not recorded, as he lived away from Verwood at that time, was Sergeant Iver Bailey, R.F.A., brother of Herbert mentioned above, who died of wounds in the Somme region of France in September 1918.

More fortunate in having all sons survive the war was the Spray family pictured left at "Westwood" in Vicarage Road. William Henry Spray, a Grocer, Rate Collector and Attendance Officer for local schools, sits centre with his wife Emily.

Their eldest son, Frank, a Master Carpenter and Joiner on the nearby Crichel Estate, also worked during the hostilities at the Dorset Lake Shipyard, Hamworthy, Poole whilst Wallace joined the Navy and Robert the Army. On a rare occasion in 1916 all the members of the family were at home together so some of the boys rode into Ringwood to call a photographer.

As the War did not touch Verwood at first hand, very little reference was made in the school log books. However, in April 1918 it was recorded that during the Easter holidays the Church School children had given a concert in the schoolroom. From the proceeds of this they had to pay a War Fund Entertainment tax of £1.18.4. However, they had made a profit of £5.12.8 from which they were allowed to buy the boys cricket bats for the forthcoming season at a cost of £1.2.0. On May 28th they held an Empire Day collection for tobacco for soldiers and on July 25th a similar one for Blinded Soldiers. At the close of the summer term in July 1919, the children were granted an extra week's holiday in celebration of "peace".

ORA PRO NOBIS

F. AUSTIN	T. FERRETT
A. BARROW	H. FERRETT
J. BARROW	W. F. INGRAM
J. BUDDEN	F. JACOBS
C. B. BAILEY	J. KEITH
A. J. BAILEY	C. KING
F. J. BAILEY	J. LANE
G. BREWER	W. MIDDLETON
N. COLBORNE	C. OXFORD
C. DYER	B. OXFORD
W. DYER	A. ROBERTS
B. DYER	E. SIMS
D. DOWLAND	D. STEELE
J. DOWLAND	T. SHERRED
H. DOWLAND	I. THORNE
R. GRACE	C. TRICKETT
C. GRACE	M. VINE
W. HIBBERD	W. WHITTY
S. HOPKINS	F. WHITTY
G. HOPKINS	C. WILSON

GRANT THEM
O LORD
ETERNAL REST
AND LET
LIGHT PERPETUAL
SHINE ON THEM.

ORA PRO NOBIS

C. W. E. ALBRAY	B. C. ORMAN
L. BARROW	E. H. PERSON
R. C. BARROW	S. W. PEARCE
S. BARROW	D. READ
M. BARRETT	R. SIMS
E. BREWER	J. SIMS
J. CHAPPELL	J. S. M. SHEARING
A. B. FOX	S. SHEARING
R. E. HARRIDGE	M. SAUNDERS
W. R. HASKELL	W. SLEE
L. K. V. KIMBERLEY	J. TOMS
C. S. KEMP	W. G. TURNER
G. J. LYNES	H. J. THORNE
J. MAN	D. J. WAREHAM

GRANT THEM
O LORD
ETERNAL REST
AND LET
LIGHT PERPETUAL
SHINE ON THEM.

Remembered peacefully in St. Michael & All Angels Parish churchyard, Verwood wherever they fell or died. The plaque left commemorates those of WWI and that right of WWII. Derek Wareham was the sole Verwood man to die in the Malayan Emergency after WWII. He was the only son of widower Mr. Arthur Wareham, village carpenter and undertaker, who gave so much valuable information to Verwood Historical Society in its early years.

W. H. BECK.　*　INDIA.

Left:　Pictured in India, Herbert Bailey with his wife Isabella and stepdaughter Dora whom he adopted. The couple had two further children, Herbert and Isabel.

Right:　Sergeant Sidney Iver Bailey who died September 1918 "For King and Country" in France during WWI. He had been married in Cheshire the previous year to Mary Kennedy.

WORLD WAR II - CASUALTIES

In addition to the Army and Navy, in this war several Verwood men joined the Royal Air Force. Amongst those who died in that service were Flying Officer Pilot Gavin John Lynes, only son of the then Vicar of Verwood; Walter Ralph Haskell, a Wing Commander at the age of 28; Squadron Leader Pilot Cyril Sydney Kemp; Aircraftman 1st Class Royston Clifford Barrow; Sergeant (Air Bomber) Robert Alfred Sims; Flight Sergeant James Gilbert Maurice (Jimmy) Shearing, a navigator on a Lancaster bomber brought down over Germany and Flight Sergeant William Slee. Those dead of the Naval contingent were Petty Officer Evan Ziph Brewer, aged 42, the oldest local casualty in either war, Able Seaman James Mann and Stoker 1st Class Maurice George Saunders. Corporal Walter George Turner and Lance Corporal Herbert John Thorne of the Corps of Military Police both died on 6th June 1943 and were buried in Verwood churchyard. Those of the Army, serving in various regiments, were buried or recorded on monuments in several widely scattered corners of the globe.

Max Barrett, the 15 year old boy who was the only civilian casualty during the war, is also recorded on the War Memorial. He died on 24th April 1944 when an incendiary bomb dropped into the bedroom of his house in Hillside Road during a night of torrential bombing. His elder brother Roy, sharing the same room, had a miraculous escape.

The village was devastated by this sad event and Ken Nicklen remembers his shock having played with Max only a few days beforehand. The Council Senior Mixed School log book records on 27th April that "Max Barrett was buried today at 2 p.m. with Girl Guides and Boy Scouts. The children who wished to attend were taken to the funeral by the teachers." It being springtime, his fellow Scouts and schoolfriends threw posies of primroses into his grave in the Parish Churchyard.

The following year, the Parish Council Minutes of 10th September 1945 record that

> **"A letter was received from Mrs. Barrow "Heatherley" Verwood on behalf of a wide circle of electors asking the Council to take a lead in placing a memorial on the grave of Max Barrett - the boy (and the only person) killed in Verwood by German air raids. After sympathetic discussion the question of the disposal of the Defence Fund and the possibility of a grant from this source was suggested and it was proposed by Mr. Craven, seconded by Mr. Thorne and carried unanimously that the Chairman be asked to submit the suggestion to the Defence Committee on winding up their accounts. The Clerk was instructed to inform Mrs. Barrow of the action taken and to express the sympathy of the Council with the views expressed in her letter."**

In accordance with these popular wishes, a monument was duly erected on the grave in the Lower Churchyard extension.

THE ARMY IN VERWOOD

Dennis and Biddy Cannell's smallholding on the corner of Ringwood and Noon Hill Roads was requisitioned for the duration of the war to become the Headquarters of the Searchlight Battery. Anti-tank divisions of the Royal Artillery were stationed in Verwood and there was a large military camp on Dewlands Common. Many men and much equipment were hidden in the forests and woods throughout the area in preparation for the D-Day invasion from south coast ports such as Poole. Thousands of American troops, including many "black soldiers", came to the area giving rise to the excitement of unfamiliarity in speech, appearance and manners.

CONFUSING THE ENEMY

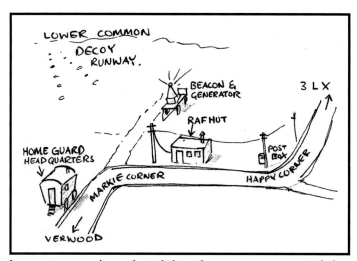

There were several genuine airfields nearby around the New Forest and it was also wished to draw attention and fire away from the large Army Petrol Depot at West Moors, further south. To this end, spotlights and a decoy runway were placed on Lower Common. When the lights were switched on enemy aircrews were meant to think they were over a genuine airfield and drop their bombs harmlessly in an unoccupied spot. However, since this was nowhere near mains electricity they were powered by generators. The RAF men who maintained the site were billeted at a house in Lake Road and, when telephoned, would cycle down to switch them on to operate the beacon and lights. Later an RAF Sergeant and airman had a base near the "runway" as shown on the map.

The first bend at Crab Orchard coming from Verwood was known as "Markie Corner" as Mark Shutler had enclosed land there from the Lower Common. The second bend for some unknown reason was known as "Happy Corner". The Home Guard used a shepherd's hut from Robert Thorne Ltd. there for their H.Q. on the left hand side of the road just before Markie Corner. Straight ahead was the gate to Lower Common and 100 yards or so beyond was a Beacon and Generator mounted on a flat bed trailer. Several enemy bombs were dropped in the area so the ploy seemingly worked unless unused ammunition was just being jettisoned before the flight home across the Channel.

AIR RAID PRECAUTIONS

The A.R.P. Wardens were an active force, supervising blackouts, stirrup pumps, gas masks, preventative measures etc. Many air raid warnings were received over the years which necessitated their attention. Pictured left, ready for duty, are Mrs. Westgate, Aubrey Barrow, an unidentified lady and Miss Jasper, the librarian.

In March 1939 Mr. W. Jeffries of Central Garage was Chief Air Raid warden and reported that Verwood and Three Legged Cross were well covered by wardens and that several well attended classes in anti-gas instruction and first aid had been held. They were also responsible for allocating shelter arrangements for children during school hours. Verwood Council School children were allocated nearby homes to run to, Verwood Church School children had to dash across the green and take refuge in a trench in the Vicarage garden whilst Three Legged Cross Church children had their desks rearranged so that they could shelter underneath them. On occasions they remained in this uncomfortable position for several hours on end. An exercise carried out early in the War found all children in place within 2 minutes of the Siren sounding. Gas Mask practice and inspection were held regularly each month and on 11th May 1944 the Three Legged Cross Church School recorded that the Mickey Mouse masks of Peter Phillips and Sidney Lacey were changed for small sized respirators.

THE HOME GUARD

The Local Defence Volunteers force was established early in 1940 attracting many too old for active service but who were eager to play their part in defending the country. Often with no proper uniform, just an LDV arm band to show their authority, they prepared to repel the enemy with whatever weapons came to hand – pitchforks, shotguns and old WWI revolvers. The Women's Institute 1984 presentation "Verwood at War" reveals some stories of those days. One man was given a rubber tube in which to insert an iron bar to fight off the invading Germans. It might be a blessing or even perhaps a pity that it was never put to the test. This growing force, snappily renamed "The Home Guard" by Winston Churchill shortly afterwards was issued with battle dress and somewhat more sophisticated weapons.

Left: George Bailey, Verwood's popular long-time barber in Home Guard uniform before joining the Royal Navy in 1942.

Verwood had two Home Guard Sections, the Northern commanded by Lt. W. Bates and the Southern, which took in Three Legged Cross, by Lt. Bendall. Each company was responsible for guarding strategic points such as the rail and road bridges and manning checkpoints at entrances to the village. At Eastworth, a wagon was positioned near the railway bridge to be pulled across the road if invasion came. The signpost at the Crossroads was necessarily removed. Dug out posts were constructed in the Stephens Castle area to observe enemy action and the Sandpits used for anti tank manoeuvres. This area was also used as a training ground for the Home Guard. George Bailey recalled that the older hands sheltered in a cabin at the bottom, sending the rookies out on patrol with the assurance that "they would be with them shortly".

In addition to their official tasks the Home Guard took part in parades such as that on Empire Day 23rd May 1941. It was celebrated by suitable Hymns, Prayers, Songs, Headmaster's Address, an address by Major A. T. Bourne R.A. and a combined march past by Pupils, A Unit of Royal Artillery, Home Guard, Scouts, Guides, Rangers, A.R.P. and A.F.S. which must have been a stirring patriotic event. They also kept up morale by organizing and assisting with parties and sports days for the village children.

Some humorous stories are told about those days. The Home Guard was called out to arrest a German pilot who had baled out when his plane came down, crashing at Gotham. In the dark early hours the Guard met someone walking down the road so the usual pleasant "Good Mornings" were exchanged and the search continued. Fortunately the police later met the wanderer, took him into custody and escorted him to the nearest POW camp. A young recruit stationed near the railway, terrified when he heard rustling in the bushes but receiving no reply to his "Halt – who goes there?", threw down his rifle and ran. The culprit was later thought to have been a cow. A short-sighted Private Brewer on point duty at Crab Orchard invited a challenged suspect to "Hang on yer to me rifle a minute, while I get me glasses out"! One entry in the duty book on a presumably otherwise uneventful night read "suspected enemy submarine spotted off Potterne Bridge".

The Home Guard was given an anti-tank gun which it was felt should be demonstrated one Sunday afternoon on the Recreation Ground. A large bonfire was built with a lump of steel in the middle to represent an oncoming German tank. Great excitement was generated by this novel form of entertainment. The gun was set up and the order given to fire. It missed. A second order was given but again it missed. It was moved even closer and finally "the tank" was hit to great cheering and much relief.

A signed copy of a photograph of the Northern Section of Verwood Home Guard

Taken outside the Pavilion on the Recreation Ground

The Southern Section of Verwood and Three Legged Cross Home Guard

WAR AND SERVICE

WOMEN AND CHILDREN

Women and children left at home together with older men and those in reserved occupations all found a useful role to play. Some ladies, amongst them Eileen Holloway and Christine Henning, bravely took on courier duty although it was by no means a pleasant experience to be cycling without lights in the middle of the Common on a pitch black night with many strangers in the vicinity. Verwood women had knitted gloves for many years and no doubt these and sewing skills were put to good use in the making of garments and comforts for the Troops as well as ekeing out clothing and linen for home use.

Verwood was fortunate in always having been an agricultural community with lifelong skills in growing vegetables, keeping livestock and catching such animals as rabbits so that everyday necessities were not in such short supply as they would have been in towns. When the Parish Council was asked if allotments should be provided, they replied that all the houses already had large gardens but they would give the matter consideration. Food and clothing parcels from relatives abroad, however, were warmly welcomed. For the rest, ration books had to supply what could not be home produced.

In October 1941 the Chairman of the Parish Council raised the question of the parish's emergency food rations and stated that these had been divided incorrectly between Verwood and Three Legged Cross, whilst the officer responsible lived at West Moors. The Rural District Council food controller was to be asked to remove anomalies. It is not clear who had received the lion's share on this occasion.

The W.I. ran a thriving Canning and Jam Making Centre at the Cookery Hut in Station Road. Children were sent or taken on foraging expeditions to provide some of the necessary fruit. On 1st September 1942 the Council School log book recorded that "at 10.30 a.m. the school was taken gathering blackberries for the Jam Making Centre. Picnic dinners were taken and all arrived back at the school at 3.45 p.m. Total gathered 124½ lbs." Another expedition on the 16th of the same month produced 84¾ lbs blackberries. "Total now 209¼ lbs". No doubt this was a useful arithmetic exercise as well as a valuable contribution to the food supply.

Random examples of other collections from the countryside were 109 lbs of rose hips, 242lbs of broom tips, 1¼ hundredweight of nettles, 3½ lbs of foxglove seeds and 3 hundredweight of horse chestnuts. These commodities were sent to local depots or further afield, the school funds receiving a modest remuneration for their efforts which could be spent on such items as library books.

Large amounts of scrap paper and books were also collected by the Wimborne Rural District Council Salvage Wagon. For the Dorset scrap metal sweep, the Salvage Officer was to be notified of accumulations of scrap metal at various places including the southwest corner of Lower Common, in the lane opposite the north end of Church road and at Messrs. Ransome's in Three Legged Cross. Railings were also taken from public and private buildings. All in all the population could justifiably feel proud that by economy, sacrifice and resourcefulness they had contributed significantly to the combined War Effort.

THE WOMEN'S LAND ARMY

Many women took on the challenge of unfamiliar jobs to free men for active service and other essential duties.

The Women's Land Army formed in the First World War was again brought into service and "Land Girls", some with no previous experience of the countryside found themselves coping bravely with unfamiliar tasks in alien surroundings.

Ethel Moody was already friendly with the Froud family of West Farm, Romford through their shared attendance at Verwood Methodist Church. They suggested that she should apply to work on their farm which she did with great enthusiasm and distinction, easily passing her agricultural examinations.

In 1944 she and the farmer's son Gerald married, commencing a long and happy life together on the farm.

Their son Roger and his wife Penny still run the farm but have converted some of the buildings into self-catering holiday cottages as "West Farm Lodges" whilst former fields are part of Crane Valley Golf Course. This is a now familiar sign of adaptation to changing agricultural patterns and leisure activities over the century.

These photographs show Ethel at work in just two of her many different capacities around West Farm in wartime

BIRDS OF PASSAGE

In the early years of the war, a canteen at the Congregational Chapel in Verwood served the 180 soldiers billeted in the village. The church was valued at £200 against the danger of bombing. Deeds and documents were handed to Lloyds Bank for safe keeping and valuables left in the care of the Treasurer. At Three Legged Cross an Officers' Mess was situated on the north side of Ringwood Road where Sandhurst Drive now lies. Gundry's Farm on the south side was requisitioned which stopped the people of that area taking their accustomed short cut through to West Moors. The path used by the Officers between the Mess and Camp became popularly known as "Drunken Alley".

A difference in culture arose on the subject of the traditional Verwood Sabbath. In the Parish Council Minutes for 13th December 1943 the Chairman, Mr. R. A. Franklin, stated that he had had verbal requests for the Recreation Ground to be used for Sunday football for Negro soldiers. After discussion it was proposed by Mr. Craven and seconded by Mr. Cannell that applications for the use of the ground at any time should be made from the Commanding Officer, and attention was drawn to the Regulations governing the use of the field by which Sunday Games are forbidden. The motion was carried unanimously.

RECREATION GROUND, VERWOOD

The subject was raised again at the Annual Parish Meeting on 27th March 1944 when the matter was discussed on a question by Mr. Stroud who was informed by the Chairman that although a regulation governing the use of the Ground forbade Sunday games he had not denied the ground to U.S. Troops. He had not been asked by these men. After discussion Mrs. Craven proposed and Mr. Mercer seconded that Sunday games be allowed on the Ground. Mr. Stainer, seconded by Mrs. Jeffreys, moved an amendment that the rules governing the ground be not set aside without specially consulting the parishioners. On being put to the vote the amendment was carried and the proposition lost.

Much more acceptably for the Verwood Sunday it was noted that the negro soldiers had lovely voices and sang beautifully in church.

On 21st November 1944 it was recorded that Peter Turner aged 5, of Edmondsham Road, attending the junior school was knocked down and injured by a lorry of the U.S.A. Army No. 229065 at 1.25 p.m. in the road near the entrance to the Market. The driver was Corporal Berndt of Q328 West Moors (Private address "The Albion" Verwood). Fortunately Peter recovered from the incident.

Many homes were also open to Evacuees from Southampton and London, all entailing the sacrifice of extra work, space and time. The local schools overflowed with the addition of this new intake. On 16th December 1940 Miss W. Fudge, Certificated Assistant teacher under the Southampton Authority, arrived at Verwood Church School to take up temporary duties on the staff, there being by then 56 evacuees on the roll. At Three Legged Cross Church School two evacuees were admitted on 25th November 1940 but five more were refused owing to lack of desks and room. However five were admitted the following April although it was still considered there was insufficient room and there were 54 children on the books. Bars of chocolate were sent from London County Council to be distributed to their evacuee children which may have been some small consolation for being so far from home.

BOMBS AND STRAY AIRCRAFT

On 3rd July 1940 at 3.05 p.m. an action Air Raid warning was received and the Council School children were dispersed to houses in the vicinity. 20 bombs were dropped and the "All Clear" was received at 3.40 p.m. After raids, unexploded bombs were discovered throughout the area and schoolboys were only too happy to be let off lessons whilst they showed the Local Authorities where they had landed. On 3rd March 1944 the Headmaster of the Council School recorded that "Some boys last night found an unexploded bomb in a wood. I allowed Michael Kearon to show P. C. Haines its position at 10 a.m."

THIS IS THE END OF THE BOMB
(TAIL-PIECE)
WHICH FELL AT
THREE CROSS
On MONDAY, JULY 1st, 1940

Two days earlier, at Three Legged Cross a bomb had fallen on Gregory's shop at the junction of Verwood and Ringwood Roads, the saved tail-piece being mounted and exhibited. Much later during the war, in July 1944, an unexploded aerial torpedo was expected to be exploded near to the Church School there at 2.30 p.m. The children were sent home at midday for the rest of the afternoon.

Disabled enemy aircraft came down in the vicinity. A Luftwaffe Focke was shot down on the Edmondsham Road near Birches Copse. Mr. Gerald Froud of West Farm, Romford found an English airman in one of his fields. He had been shot down by mistake whilst returning from a mission but was fortunately unharmed.

Miss Gertie Sims was running Eastworth Farm whilst her brothers were away, with the aid of a dairyman, a Polish tractor driver and some Land Girls. The cows were kept in the field on the north side of Station Road. One day Miss Sims, Mrs. Tennant the Stationmaster's wife and another helper, were out in the field pulling up docks when two enemy planes came across and machine gunned them. There were bullets flying all around and they had to dive under the hedge for cover.

On the night of the worst bombing raid Miss Sims was visiting Mrs. Clarke the policeman's wife at the Police House in Ringwood Road when the bombs started falling and so she immediately rushed home. A cow hit by a bomb went mad with pain and all the other cows went mad at the sight and smell of blood. She took off her jacket and walked around in a circle to keep the other cows from the injured one. A porter at the station who lived opposite heard her shout and fetched other members of the family. The cow ran off and died so they shovelled earth over it to hide it from the other cows. Ginger, one of their horses was also killed by a bomb.

This was the night of 23/24th April 1944 which stood out in everyone's mind as the most terrifying experience. A lady who lived on Station Road at the time reported that as a child she had watched from her bedroom window with a fascinated mixture of fear and excitement as the bombs rained down just a few yards away. Several houses were destroyed or severely damaged with people rendered destitute and homeless. It was reported that the Assistant Master of the Council School, Mr. Stride, did yeoman service, one house being saved by his efforts and prompt action.

These are but a few examples of the number of air raids which Verwood and Three Legged Cross experienced over these years. Obviously there was no comparison with the loss of life and damage suffered by cities and manufacturing towns but a frightening personal experience none the less in the midst of an otherwise quiet rural area.

WARTIME DECISIONS

In 1943 the Rural District Council asked the Parish Council to state its need for Post-War Housing for the working classes. They replied that, owing to war marriages, sixteen houses were needed in the whole parish, twelve in Verwood proper and four in Three Legged Cross. Four houses needed demolition, two in Moorlands Road, Verwood and two opposite the Travellers Rest owned by Mr. Robbins. No houses needed reconditioning and none were overcrowded. The estimated future need for housing generally was 8 houses in the whole parish, six at Verwood and two at Three Legged Cross. In their wildest dreams they could not have imagined the size of the two communities some sixty years later!

A tricky problem to do with local initiative occurred when at the Parish Council Meeting on 19th June 1944 the Clerk reported that a cow had been tethered in the Recreation Ground. After discussion, Mr. Franklin proposed and Mr. Barrow seconded that a letter be written to Mr. Nicklen, the owner of the cow, asking him to refrain from such action and also requesting him to tether his goats so that they will not be able to cause damage to the Recreation Ground hedges. This was agreed unanimously.

VICTORY

Victory in Europe or "VE" Day was celebrated nationwide on Tuesday 8th May 1945, that and the following day being declared Public Holidays. At Verwood Council Senior Mixed School, pupils assembled as usual at 9 a.m. on the Tuesday when a Thanksgiving Service of Praise and Song was held during which the Headmaster, Mr. Strawbridge, gave an address. Milk was served and then all adjourned to the Recreation Ground. Sports, run from 4 to 7 p.m. were organized by the teachers and funded by public subscription through the Parish Council. On 14th June as part of the ongoing celebrations all the children of the village of school age attended a tea party and entertainment in the Recreation Ground provided by the Parish Council from 5p.m. to 7 p.m. On 31st October the Council School closed at 3.40 p.m. until Nov 7th for the mid term break and celebrations of VJ days for the Victory over Japan.

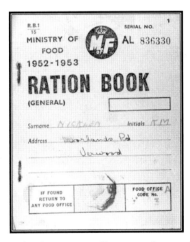

The following January, the school log book recorded that bananas had appeared in the shops for children after an absence of five years. It is hard to imagine now what excitement this caused, especially for parents eager to explain this "new" fresh fruit to somewhat bewildered younger children. Rationing, of course, continued for several years after the war.

For the Victory Day Celebrations on June 8th 1946, Colonel Winterscale informed the Council that the Three Legged Cross children would be conveyed to Verwood to make a united day. After paying for transport, any surplus funds would help defray the cost of entertainment. Children were to bring their own drinking vessels. Lemonade was to be provided and the parents asked to contribute cakes. There were to be sports and Mr. Garnham suggested that Mr. Stickland "The Wessex Wizard" of West Moors be asked to give an entertainment. It is not recorded, however, that he appeared to make things disappear and in the event the celebrations were marred by rain so all the children assembled in the Council School to be entertained by song and chorus. Mr. H. C. Barrow, Chairman of the Parish Council gave an address and Ice Cream was provided by Mr. W. E. Twitchen of the grocer's shop, the latter treat no doubt the highlight of the proceedings.

According to the Dorset County Chronicle, when over 7,000 Home Guard troops from all parts of Britain marched in the final parade before the King, the proud representatives of Verwood were L/Cpl E.F. Shearing, Privates V.A. Bailey and A.F. Lockyer.

MEMORIAL

The subject of a new Village Hall had been under discussion for a number of years prior to the Second World War. Many fund raising activities were held and a proportion of the Carnival funds allocated. By March 1937 £70 had been raised and the committee's activities were regularly reported to the Parish Council. By 1943 the funds stood at £384.2.8. It seemed natural to suggest, therefore, that the proposed building should become a Memorial Hall and as the Verwood branch of the British Legion was also planning to build a Clubhouse a suggestion was made that these could be combined. However this was vetoed by the Legion on the grounds that they wished their hall to be for members only.

Fund raising continued and in 1955 the New Hall Committee became the Memorial Hall Committee. The Parish Council was appointed its Trustees and with various local representatives formed the Management Committee. After considering various options, it was decided that a "Reema" Hall be erected on the Recreation Ground "which is the Memorial to those who fell during 1914-1918". Officially opened on Saturday 9th May 1959, the Hall was justly hailed as "A Great Achievement" by those who had laboured twenty-three years to see it come to fruition.

The Memorial Hall under construction

At the end of the war, the British Legion also wanted to discuss the possibility of having the War Memorial resited to a more prominent position. However, it remains at its original location in the parish churchyard. In later years a marble monument commemorating the fallen was erected at the entrance to the Recreation Ground, later removed to the newly landscaped Ferrett Green where it provides a focal point at the Remembrance Day parade.

THE SOMERLEY LAND SALE

In July 1919 the 4th Earl of Normanton, Sidney James Agar, sold off 7,650 acres of the outlying portions of his Somerley Estate. This included much of north and mid Verwood as well as an area stretching from Ebblake to Woolsbridge. It was a turning point in the fortunes of many Verwood folk who were able to buy their own sitting tenancies on houses, farms and work places thus becoming property holders in their own right. Several astute businessmen were able to buy a substantial acreage of agricultural and building land together with sand, gravel and clay deposits. Fred Sims bought Eastworth Farm, Sidney Palmer much of Boveridge Heath including the sandpits, Fred Shearing the land, house and buildings on which his forge and cycle repair shop stood at the Crossroads, Job Brewer substantial land to the north of the Crossroads amongst other examples. Also included were the Station Brickworks and the Tileyard over the road as well as the Restynge House in Ringwood Road and the Conservative Hall on the corner.

The prospectus is a masterpiece of estate agents' rhetoric – "Charming Building Site", "Capital Rough-cast Cottage", "Picturesque Cottage, Garden and Orchard", "Attractive Small Holding", "Valuable and Compact Farm", all elaborated on in descriptive style.

One would imagine that the sale might have sparked an immediate building boom in Verwood but where were the people to come from to inhabit so many new houses as could be constructed? Although Ringwood and Manor Roads and later Station Road filled out along a ribbon development, most of the remainder remained rural until recent years. The descendants of some of those shrewd purchasers have benefitted financially in recent years now the demand for building land has increased dramatically and the price per acre soared.

The Auction Lots described on the following pages lead us back to a scene of barns, piggeries and thatched cow sheds, very different from the centre of Verwood we know today.

An Attractive Small Holding

In the Village of Verwood,

INCLUDING

A Cottage, Buildings, Garden, Orchard and Paddocks,

The whole comprising an Area of

6 Acres, 3 Roods, 4 Perches,

Portions of which form

Admirable Building Sites.

The COTTAGE is good, being Brick Built and Slated, and Part Thatched, and contains :—Living Room, Parlour, Dairy, Pantry, Two Bedrooms, and Box Room.

The BUILDINGS include a Barn, Piggeries, Timber and Thatched Cow Shed, and a Good Well.

The LAND includes Five Paddocks and an Arable Field, with a well planted Orchard and Garden.

SCHEDULE.

No. on Ord. Survey.	Description.	Area.
28	Pasture ...	·874
27	Arable ...	·654
30	Pasture ...	·402
31	Pasture ...	·432
32	Cottage, Garden, Orchard, etc.	·542
33	Pasture ...	1·124
Pt. 18	Rough Pasture ...	2·750
	TOTAL ACRES ...	6·778

This Holding, with other Land, is now let to **Mrs. J. Read.**

Possession will be given on Completion of the Purchase.

The Timber is included in the Purchase.

Outgoings.—Nil.

GROUND RENT and REVERSION

Being Site of Club and Premises known as

"Ye Restynge House,"

A Brick and Tiled Building, which, with **Two Roods of Land,** is in the Occupation of the Trustees of
" Ye Restynge House," on a Lease of 99 Years from 29th September, 1906, at a Ground Rent of
15s. per annum.

Outgoings.—Nil.

The Parish Church, through the Trustees, purchased the Restynge House in Ringwood Road

Valuable Accommodation or Building Land

CONTAINING

4 Acres, 1 Rood, 22 Perches,

Near Verwood Green, consisting of

GOOD PASTURE and USEFUL ARABLE LAND.

This Lot is now Let with **Baker's Farm,** and part is utilised as a **Recreation Ground.** It is situated in the centre
of the village of Verwood and has an excellent position and Road Frontage.

Possession will be given on Completion of Purchase.

There is no Timber.

Outgoings.—Nil.

Job Brewer purchased land including that used as a Recreation Ground after WWI
An indenture between himself and Lord Normanton dated 5th January 1920 sealed the transaction.
On 4 December 1920 he conveyed the Recreation Ground plot to the Parish Council
for the sum of £300 raised for the purpose by public subscription

COMPACT SMALL HOLDING

Near **Verwood Church,** comprising

House, Useful Buildings

AND

18 Acres and 35 Perches of Productive Land.

The **HOUSE** is Plaster, Thatched and Tiled, with Lean-to, and contains Wash House, Kitchen,
Sitting Room, Dairy and Cellar, and Three Bedrooms.
The **BUILDINGS** are Timber and Thatched, and include Barn and Boxes.
The **LAND** adjoins the Premises, and consists of conveniently sized Enclosures of Good Arable and
Valuable Pasture, as described in the following

SCHEDULE.

No. on Ord. Survey.	Description.	Area.
340	Cottage, Garden, Yard and Buildings	˙402
342	Arable	2˙561
343	Pasture	1˙136
380	Arable	3˙673
379	Pasture	1˙758
381	Pasture	3˙374
438	Arable	1˙429
429	Pasture	1˙568
426	Pasture	˙835
427	Rough Pasture	1˙485
	TOTAL ACRES ...	18˙221

The Lot, with other Land, is in the Occupation of **Mr. Henry Bailey.** Vacant Possession will be given on Completion
of Purchase.
The Purchaser shall, in addition to the Purchase-money, take and pay the sum of **£29** for the Timber standing on the Lot.
Outgoings.—Tithe £3 12s. 3d., commuted amount.

POND FARM

Henry Bailey presumably bought his holding. Bounded to the west by Margards Lane, part of the land today contains Glenwood Road, Lancaster Drive, Burley Close, Keswick Way, Penrith Close and Coniston Close.

The Verwood & Gotham Brick Works

Well situate adjoining the L. & S.W. Railway Station and Sidings at Verwood,
only about 18 miles by Rail from Bournemouth and Salisbury, together with

21 Acres 1 Roods, 8 Perches,

AND THE

Valuable Beds of Brick Earth Underlying,

Which manufactures exceptionally good coloured and durable Bricks and Tiles.

On this Lot have been erected

Large Brick and Tile Works

Of Two Floors carried on Iron Girders, with Boarded Floors and Corrugated Iron Roof; containing
Engine Room, Workshops, Boiler House and Range of Three Large Drying Sheds, with Brick
Walls; **Large Hoffman Kiln** with Twenty-two Chambers; **Two Brick and Tiled Offices** and
Open Scotch Kiln.

Except **2½ Acres In Hand,** the Property is now Let on Lease for 40 Years from 31st December, 1913, to the
Verwood and Gotham Brick and Tile Company, subject to certain conditions and observations, with other
Lands, at fixed Rents and Royalties, the Apportioned Rent on this Lot being **£75·1s. 0d.** per annum and Royalties.

The Purchaser shall, in addition to the Purchase-money, take and pay the sum of **£35** for the Timber on this Lot.

The Purchaser of this Lot shall Fence off the Roadway on the West side of Field Ordnance No. 195 situate between the
Wood No. 194 and Field No. 294.

SCHEDULE.

No. on Ord. Survey.	Description.	Area.
Pt. 195	Brick Works and Land	2·227
196	Brick Works and Land	7·137
293	Dewlands Copse ... ... **In Hand**	2·273
294	Brick Works and Land	8·506
296	Brick Works and Land	·896
297	Plantation ... ... **In Hand**	·263
	TOTAL ACRES ...	21·302

Outgoings.—Nil.

The Station Brickworks became a Mushroom Farm after World War II then the buildings were demolished to make way for Lesser's Building Systems. It is now the site of Albion Way

There were countless other lots of similar description in the same sale, a very few still remaining today as thatched cottages and early 20th century houses though with reduced surrounding acreage. Many of the open fields and woods have now been built over to accommodate the ever growing population of our erstwhile Village now designated a Town.

DOWN MEMORY LANE

BAKER'S FARM IN STATION ROAD
LOOKING TOWARDS THE CROSSROADS

The photograph was probably taken in the late 1920s after the buildings around the Crossroads had been erected. Parts of the farmhouse and barns remained until the 1970s though it had long been abandoned as a dwelling. The sycamore trees remained arched over the road until developments began on either side. To the left is now Berkeley Close whilst on the right are the Fire and Police Stations then a Doctors' Surgery complex with Vet's and Chemist. In the fields behind lie the Day Care Centre, "The Hub" and a block of flats.

Please join us in a nostalgic stroll around more scenes of Verwood and Three Legged Cross which have now vanished or changed beyond recognition.

AN AERIAL VIEW OF VERWOOD IN THE EARLY 1970s

TAKEN FROM ABOVE MANOR ROAD LOOKING NORTH

The photograph is centred on the Crossroads. The Parish Churchyard is seen bottom left with Eastworth at the top. The Recreation Ground lies to the right whilst a still rural Station Road leads off left centre. The fields are now taken up by housing and other private and public developments.

STATION ROAD – THE RAILWAY BRIDGE

The road snaking towards Cranborne before it was realigned to pass in front of the Albion Hotel on the route it had taken before the railway came. Foot passengers reached the station via a flight of steps. Children used to leave their bicycles under the trees on the left and still find them there when they returned from school by train. The iconic red telephone box is another reminder of a past way of life before the advent of mobile phones.

ROMFORD BRIDGE

Over the railway bridge we come to the River Crane, the road leading on to West Farm on the left and East Farm on the right. The ford which was in use both before and after the bridge was built can be clearly seen alongside. Here at the parish boundary, we leave behind the now urban sprawl of Verwood. The true story is told of an agitated delivery driver unable to find his destination. He had to be told that he was well over a hundred miles away from the better known Romford in Essex!

STATION ROAD LOOKING WEST

Back in the village at Baker's Farm, the road meanders in the direction of Romford and Cranborne.

DOWN MEMORY LANE

ACROSS THE COMMON

Dewlands Way looking up the hill towards the village from the site of the present "Bridleways". The long low building behind the oak tree was once the Shearing's pottery.

This road is now lined with houses, surfaced and on a bus route!

Dave Haskell of Does Farm with his horse on a still rural part of Dewlands Common.

Mrs. Haskell used to bake biscuits and make lemonade to sell to picnic and bathing parties going along the lane to the pool at Does Hatches. This welcome service turned an outing into a treat.

Margards Lane looking up towards Church Hill. It remained a rough track onto the Common until houses and bungalows were built either side in the 1970s.

The house on the right then named "St. Anne's" was where Miss Violet Tennyson lived after her retirement from St. Gabriel's Orphanage.

DOWN MEMORY LANE

AT THE CROSSROADS

A cart travels from Edmondsham Road into Manor Road at a time when there no buildings around except for the Unionist Hall on the north-east corner. In the right foreground is the land which used to be the claypit for the pottery and is now Ferrett Green.

Looking to the right of the above picture, the sandpits at Stephen's Castle are visible on the horizon. Very shortly afterwards "The Parade" and "The Restynge House" would be built alongside the hall, obscuring this view.

The Hills, Verwood.

CROSS ROAD, VERWOOD.

Later, looking towards the east. The Chemist's shop, just out of sight on the left, the Newsagents and "The Parade" have now been built. On the right is Shearing's garage offering Esso petrol. The cycle repair shop at the front of the garage can just be seen beneath the sign.

MANOR ROAD LOOKING NORTH

This photograph of a horseman stopping to talk to a group of children, probably on their way home from the nearby Church School, was taken from around the southern entrance to Church Hill. The large oak tree remained for many years despite the road increasing in width and traffic. It stood where there is now a pedestrian entrance to Cartref Close, the supermarket and Leisure Centre.

MANOR ROAD LOOKING SOUTH

Taken in the early 20th century when the horse and cart was still the normal form of transport but modern family housing had started to be built along some of Verwood's roads. The houses are well spread out with ample room for a large garden. Today, many of these gardens have been divided to make room for additional dwellings, leaving just a small curtilage around the original house. These houses stand just south of Glenwood Road and are now numbered 68 and 72 Manor Road. The oak tree under which the girl is sitting still remains.

TRICKETT'S COTTAGE IN MANOR ROAD

Verwood's first official Post Office established 1895 when Mr. John Trickett, then aged 59, became Postmaster. The business side was probably housed in the extension on the right. The huge "Monkey Puzzle" trees were a feature of the front garden for many years.

THE OLD POST OFFICE IN MANOR ROAD

John Trickett's son Ivor then moved the Post Office a few houses further north to a brick built house near the entrance to the Church School. In this photograph, "Verwood Post Office" is painted above the shop front on the left. Later the Post Office moved to Vicarage Road and this became Bryer Ash Coal Depot under the management of Mr. Ira Henning, the house being named "Penarth".

LAKE ROAD IN NEWTOWN

The creation of "Newtown" was a late 19th century "building boom" with large plots carved out of the North Common, south of Black Hill and stretching across to Potterne on both sides of what is now Newtown Road. The line of present Newtown Lane had long been encroached but land on the other side developed into Lake Road. Again, as was the Verwood custom, spacious grounds were allotted to each property. With the development of the local brick industry came a change of building material from the traditional cob although such cottages were built in this material and style well into the twentieth century.

Lake Road, like so many others in Verwood, was unsurfaced for most of its life and only made up in 1976. There are a decreasing number of the gravelled roads, frequently punctuated by large potholes, along which cars, bicycles and pedestrians had to precariously navigate. Moneyfly Road and part of Margards Lane serve to remind us of what the majority of surfaces, apart from the main through roads, used to be like up until the late twentieth century.

RINGWOOD ROAD LOOKING EAST

The main thoroughfare from Ringwood to Cranborne was still unsurfaced when these three brand new, matching family homes were built on the south side of the road in the early twentieth century. The children, no doubt curious about the photographer, add a period touch to the scene. The site of the Bethel Chapel, built in 1931, is next to the gate in the near right of the picture. The brick house beyond, now replaced by a modern dwelling, contained "Henry's Stores" on the corner of Newtown Road.

RINGWOOD ROAD LOOKING WEST

Across the road brick houses begin to be interspersed with earlier cob dwellings. The prominent white, thatched cottage was that first lived in by William Sims born Moor Crichel about 1782. He came to Verwood as a young man and with his first wife, Sarah Bailey, had nine children, several of whom married into other village families thus founding a dynasty still very much in evidence today.

RINGWOOD ROAD LOOKING TOWARDS THE NORTH-WEST

This "Birds-Eye View" must have been taken from the top of the Manor Brickworks chimney unless an early form of aerial photography was in operation. Despite the ribbon development along the main road, it is still a very rural scene with fields spreading behind the houses and cottages.

RINGWOOD ROAD STORES

The grocery shop belonging to Jesse and Mary Ann Shearing and their descendants is just out of picture to the lower right on the scene above. The sign board surrounding the shop front in the ground floor window can just be seen above the hedge. The lower storey was later extended to the pavement and remains so, much updated, as Verwood's main shopping outlet at the east end of the town. Today it is sited close to traffic lights on the busy Black Hill road junction.

CRAB ORCHARD

The Gamekeeper's Cottage later named Rushmore Farm. Mark Thorne was the keeper here in 1901 working for his brother Sam of Manor Farm. Their father James had also been a gamekeeper. Mark had spent several years of his career working in Almeley, Herefordshire before returning home to Verwood. The house contained the family living rooms on the right and working quarters on the left.

HOLLY TREE FARMHOUSE ON RINGWOOD ROAD, THREE LEGGED CROSS

The marks of the cob rearings by which the house was built can clearly be seen left of the doorway.

WOOLSBRIDGE

Woolsbridge at the far eastern end of Three Legged Cross marks the county boundary with Hampshire. Here the River Crane flowing from Verwood becomes the Moors River before joining the Stour at Blackwater near the junction on the A338 Spur Road leading to Hurn and Christchurch. The ford has long gone out of use and the bridge which bore a transportation warning sign is no more.

THREE LEGGED CROSS, DORSET.

GREGORY'S STORE

The road rises over the former railway bridge towards Horton whilst the signpost points to Verwood at the end of our journey "Down Memory Lane".

THE REUNION TEA PARTY

On 15th February 1988 Verwood Historical Society hosted a Tea Party at Hillside School for those who had attended Verwood Schools during the 1920s. Although several still lived in the village, others came from far away to be reunited with their fellow children from that era. It is to these and other past and present villagers that we owe this record of bygone days.

Ladies' maiden names given as known at school with married surname in brackets

BACK ROW: 1. Owen Sims   2. Percy Sims   3. Christine Henning (Stratton)   4. Unidentified   5. Maurice Stratton   6. Joe Ferrett   7. Fred "Pablo" Bailey   8. Frank Stone   9. Reg Cox   10. Tom Barrow   11. Clive Thorne   12. Daphne Sims (Shearing)   13. Vic Batten   14. Joyce King (Duncan)   15. Doug Thorne   16. Grace Davis (Atyeo)   17. Iris King (Martin)   18. Norman King

3RD ROW: 1. Unidentified   2. Charlie Shearing   3. Eric Shearing   4. Harold Ferrett   5. Arthur Spencer   6. Arthur Poolman   7. Harold Middleton   8. (Cecil) Arthur "Sammy" Barrow   9. Sybil Middleton (Macey)   GAP   10. Ron Bailey   11. Alec Shearing   12. Monsell Shearing

2ND ROW: 1. George Bailey   2. Rosemarie Webb   3. Annie Palmer (Shearing)   4. Elsie Brewer (Bailey)   5. Doreen Haskell   6. Ruth Henning (Scammell, Pearson)   7. Gwen Holloway (Brewer, Penfold)   8. Unidentified   9. Annie Day (Manston)   10. Irene Bugler (Webber)   11. Joan Sims (Wilcox)   12. Unidentified   13. Eileen Holloway (Smith)   14. Ruth Shearing (Thorne)   15. Aubrey Barrow

FRONT ROW: 1. Blanche Thorne (Kirk)   2. Gwen Thompson (Reeks)   3. Gladys Thorne (Case)   4. Arthur Bailey   5. Unidentified   6. Len Sims   7. Maud Haskell (Brewer)   8. Lily Brewer (Trowbridge)   9. Grace Stickland (Seymour)   10. Marjorie Oliver (Davies)   11. Joan Bugler (Steel)   12. Neville Brewer

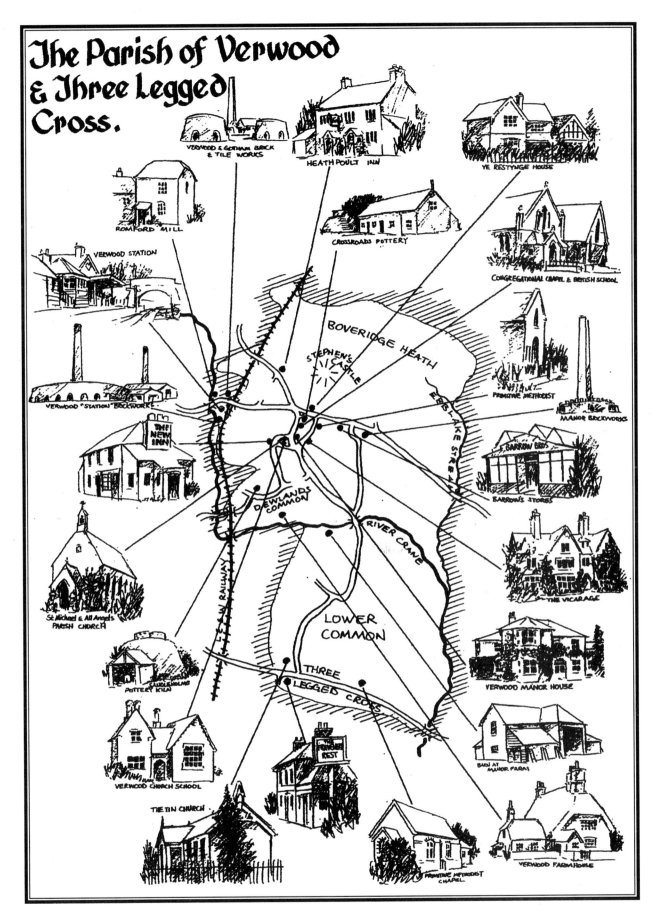

AN ILLUSTRATED MAP OF VERWOOD FEATURES

DESIGNED AND DRAWN BY CLIVE DANIELS

BIBLIOGRAPHY

Hutchins History of Dorset, 3rd Edition, Vol. III. Rev. J. Hutchins, M.A.

Chronicles of Cranborne. Dr. T. Wake Smart

Unpublished Thesis. Pamela Reeks. 1968

Unpublished Thesis. Jane Hood.   1978

Kelly's Directories of Dorset

Somerset and Dorset Notes & Queries, Vol III. Printed 1893

Dorset Year Book. 1929

D.C.C. Planning Brief for Verwood. 1968

Census Returns for Verwood and Cranborne

Cranborne and Verwood Parish Registers

Verwood Tithe Map and Apportionment, 1847

Minutes of Wimborne & Cranborne Rural District Council

Minutes of Verwood Parish Council

Minutes of Wimborne and Cranborne Union (Workhouse)

Verwood Church School Log Books

Verwood Council School Log Books

Three Legged Cross Church School Log Books

FURTHER READING

St. Michael & All Angels, Verwood
A Guide and History of the Parish Church   **Jill Coulthard Pub. 2001   Available from Church**

In a Small Village
Verwood Road Evangelical Chapel   **Ken Orman   Pub. 2004   Available from Church**